GRA
AN

Grain Contracts and Arbitration

FOR SHIPMENTS FROM THE UNITED STATES AND CANADA

By
ALBERT SLABOTZKY

LONDON
LLOYD'S OF LONDON PRESS LTD.
LEGAL PUBLISHING & CONFERENCES DIVISION
26–30 Artillery Lane, Bishopsgate
London E1 7LX
1984

ISBN 0–907432–88–3

Printed in Great Britain by
St Edmundsbury Press, Bury St Edmunds, Suffolk

To my Wife Aida, condition precedent and warranty of our mutual and several happiness and well-being.

Foreword

We are bound, by hallowed precedent, to start out with a formal, legal definition of a contract. We cite from a most respected authority, the *Restatement of Contracts*,[1] issued by the American Law Institute:

> "A contract is a promise or a set of promises for the breach of which the law gives a remedy, or the performance of which the law in some way recognizes a duty."

A cynic might remark that the legal mind seems to put breaches ahead of performance, but this would be a hasty and unjust verdict.

For our own non-legal purposes, we shall define a contract as the mutual undertakings of buyer and seller, embodied in a written document spelling out their rights and obligations and the means of recourse for breaches. In the simplest terms, contracts tell what each party *must* do, what each party *may* do, and what happens "if they don't".

This book reviews in some detail the provisions of grain contracts and, in particular, those of the standard forms most important to exporters of grain and soyabeans from the United States and Canada, viz., GAFTA 27 and 30, FOSFA 24 and NAEGA 2. (These acronyms refer to the professional groups which drew up the contracts and which are described in Chapter 3. GAFTA stands for The Grain and Feed Trade Association, Ltd., London; FOSFA for F.O.S.F.A. [Federation of Oils, Seeds, and Fats Associations] International, London; and NAEGA, for North American Export Grain Association, Inc., Washington, D.C.) From these standard contracts, we have attempted to draw general principles applicable to all international grain contracts. For the benefit of those who have little acquaintance with such subjects as ocean freight and letters of credit, we have presented their basic elements in some detail, before relating them to commodity sales.

We have aimed for a practical exposition of our subject, but have not shrunk from a study of the legal background to supply insights into the intent and the formulation of contractual terms. The cases cited are generally those of English tribunals which exercised broad

[1] *Restatement*, *Second*, "Contract", §1.

powers of review over arbitration awards on questions of law under the Arbitration Act of 1950; the Arbitration Act of 1979 greatly restricted this access to the courts, but important cases are still heard. Such a body of construction does not exist in the United States, where grain arbitration awards are practically immune from legal challenge on their merits.

We hope that this book will find some favor with experienced grain people as well as with neophytes, and that readers will be encouraged to pursue their inquiry into this interesting subject.

In American usage, the buyer and the seller are referred to as "he". Our English cousins, with uncanny prescience, have, it seems, always tended to the neutral "they". In this book, we have made much of the need for contract language to remain abreast of developments; it would be inconsistent as well as ungracious of us not to take account of a significant social trend: we have adopted the neutral "it" when writing about the parties to an agreement.

I am indebted to several colleagues for their kind advice. Mr Jack Berg, distinguished maritime arbitrator, obliging mentor and steadfast friend, first made me aware of the trend toward "superconsolidations" in commodity and maritime arbitrations. Upon reading the typescript, he gave me excellent suggestions. Dr Ted Rice, who heads Continental Grain Company's Research Department, favored me with invaluable counsel. Mr Jim Reed and Mr Mike Feiler, also of Continental Grain, provided guidance and encouragement.

New York ALBERT SLABOTZKY
January 1984

Contents

CHAPTER 1

The Importance of Contracts

The Bible tells us that, smitten by Laban's younger daughter, Jacob agreed to do seven years' labour in the fields for her hand. After this time he expectantly went to claim his bride, but Laban deviously contrived to make him toil another seven years. Through this experience, Jacob must have learned a lot about human nature; he should also have learned that he might have fared better had the agreement with Laban been put down clearly in writing. In our time, he might also have to think of securing the young lady's consent freely given, and possibly of hiring an attorney to draw up the contract!

Contracts are not only more complicated than in Biblical days, they are becoming more so with every passing year, at least as regards grain transactions. Poorly drafted instruments create the risk of large losses, even if there is little danger of being forced to work the fields for seven years. Two decades ago, not much attention was paid to the technicalities of grain contracts. The contracts were simple documents by today's standards and the trade looked to the substance of agreements, rather than to the fine print, on the premise, perhaps, that the letter killeth. Unfortunately, this idyllic state could not outlast the roller-coaster of prices which began in 1972. The temptation to use technicalities to avoid or postpone insolvency, or simply to obliterate a loss or to reap a tidy gain, proved irresistible to a few. It seems that when their interests are substantially involved there are some firms which achieve prodigies of ingenuity in finding loopholes in contracts. The Chairman of FOSFA's Vegetable/ Maritime Oil Committee said in an address in 1979:

> "We are in a world where in our daily business lives we are encountering more and more devious minds which think the way to do business is by 'sharp' practice and it is very sad that our business, so clear for so many years, is now being tainted by this sort of person. Please, I request of you to remember that the commodity business and our own in particular can be kept clean in these very difficult days by reminding oneself continuously of the well-known emblem in the Queen's Room of the Baltic on which the motto is emblazoned 'My word—my bond'. Let that continue to be our motto . . ."[1]

[1] *FOSFA Newsletter*, No. 42, February 1980.

Today, all participants in the grain trade pay rather close heed to the language of their contracts, if only in self-defence. In the earlier, carefree days, a seller of grain c.i.f. a European port had faithfully performed its end of the deal, except for having overlooked sending the buyer a notice of appropriation; this is an advice identifying the contract and the details of shipment made thereunder, viz., contract number, vessel name, bill of lading date, quantity and description of the goods loaded. The contract required the notice to be sent within a stipulated number of days after the bill of lading date. Unaware of the slip, the seller had the shipping documents prepared and presented to the buyer for payment. The buyer refused to honour the drawing but gave no reasons for this action. Upon inquiry from the seller, the buyer identified the error, but by then the vessel was well on its way to the destination. The seller had never had to face this particular problem, and felt compelled to refer it to a London attorney, as the contract had been made subject to English law. Today, anyone conversant with contracts would know the answer automatically: English courts have held that failure to give a notice of appropriation within the required deadline entitles the buyer to reject the documents and to call the seller in default. A loss in the difference between the contract price and the market value suffered by the buyer is recoverable from the seller. Not observing the niceties of what may appear to be routine advices can become the source of much grief and prejudice.

Another interesting example of a fine contractual point is related by an old-timer in the business. In this incident, which occurred about the time of the Second World War, the seller of a "full and complete cargo" of grain decided that it would be a good idea to send a 100 lb. bag of another kind of grain in the vessel, as a large sample for a customer at the port of destination. When the vessel arrived at its destination, the buyer refused to take delivery of the cargo, claiming that it was not a full and complete cargo of the commodity purchased, the additional bag having been placed in a hold on top of the grain appropriated under the contract. The story goes that a settlement was eventually reached between the parties.

In the "old" days, youngsters starting out in the grain business were made to spend long hours poring over the language of contracts, as the most logical introduction to the grain trade. A thorough knowledge of contracts brings with it a solid comprehension of the various elements of execution and of the techniques of trading as well.

For example, the commodity description in a contract may refer to the U.S. Grain Standards Act, or the Canada Grain Act. To understand what this means, one has to know something about what the grading factors are, which agencies perform this service, etc. If the contract is for delivery c.i.f. Rotterdam, it is necessary to understand the obligations of seller and buyer in this type of transaction: what each must do (or arrange to be done), and for what costs each is responsible; some acquaintance with ocean freight is essential. If payment is by letter of credit, one will wish to understand how this method of payment is carried out. We have by no means exhausted the list with these few examples. A good grounding also includes some knowledge of the general principles of commercial law.

The contract contains all the material points of the bargain struck between the seller and the buyer, as well as guidelines for the interpretation of these points. Mastering these is a *sine qua non*, followed or accompanied by a study of the custom and usage of the trade.

The contracts in use today have a long history. It is no coincidence that those in greatest use world-wide are English. In 1663, a Corn Law was passed setting "a duty of 5s. 4d. per quarter on wheat imported from abroad when the home price did not exceed 48s. Correspondingly heavy rates were laid down to control the import of other kinds of grain."[2] The Common Market levies were thus anticipated by some three centuries. Corn laws were amended as needs and political pressures dictated; but they were completely repealed in 1849, and England became a substantial importer of grain, which, by the way, they persist in calling "corn"! These heavy imports are thought to have assisted greatly in the industrialisation of the country. Buying and selling of grain was carried on in the Baltic Exchange in London; and in about 1871 the Liverpool Corn Trade Association was created.[3] In 1878 there came into being the London Corn Trade Association, the forerunner of The Grain and Feed Trade Association Ltd., which is very much a going concern today. The historical development of English contracts explains why transactions between Argentine shippers and Italian importers are made under the basic conditions of an English contract, and subject to English law.

[2] Asa Briggs, "Corn Laws", *Encyclopaedia Britannica*, 1970, Vol. 6, p. 512.

[3] Arthur Barker, *The British Corn Trade*, Pitmans' Common Commodities and Industries (London: Pitman & Son, Ltd.—undated), p. 68.

The United States has long been a substantial grain exporter; and over the years, has evolved the most comprehensive and the most satisfactory f.o.b. vessel contract for grain.

CHAPTER 2

How Purchases are Made

A distinction may be made between transactions involving two commercial firms, and those in which one of the parties is a governmental agency or a formal association of buyers.

Contracts entered into by two private companies are negotiated directly by them; or, more frequently, they are made through an independent broker. Sometimes, there are two brokers to a transaction, one in each party's country; the co-brokers operate under an agreement between them. The transactions may be concluded over the telephone in a very short time, since the parties need to bargain only on a few terms, such as quantity, commodity description (e.g., U.S. No. 3 Yellow Corn, maximum 15% moisture), price and delivery basis (e.g., U.S. $100 per metric ton f.o.b. vessel Mississippi River Ports excluding Baton Rouge and New Orleans Public Elevator), time of delivery (e.g., November 1–15, 1982) and payment (e.g., by telegraphic transfer against presentation of documents in the City of ——). For f.o.b. vessel sales, for instance, other terms would be included such as pre-advice period, carrying charges and possibly a load rate guarantee (e.g., 5,000 metric tons per WWDSHEX, demurrage/despatch $5,000/$2,500). In addition to items such as these, the parties also agree on "standard contract language". These standard terms are simply the "small print" governing the fulfilment of the contract.

In Rotterdam and other active markets, offers are submitted daily by exporters through agents and brokers, valid up to the opening of the futures market in North America on the following business day. In places where purchases are made more sporadically, offers are given when they are requested. Sales of grain, oilseeds and related products from the United States are generally made by the private trade, even when government financing or guarantees are involved. Exports of wheat and barley from Canada are controlled by the Canadian Wheat Board. According to Canadian Wheat Board Commissioner W. Esmond Jarvis approximately 80% of the CWB's sales are made directly to buyers overseas, mostly governmental agencies.

The balance is sold to "accredited exporters" of the Board, which resell the grain to foreign customers[1]; these are commercial sales, with contract terms ruling for the markets in question.

The broker, if there is one, issues the written contract in letter-form recording the agreement between buyer and seller. If no broker is involved, it is expected that the seller will establish the contract. Some members of the trade have been issuing contracts with the aid of computers, and FOSFA International accommodates this procedure with handy forms and seals. The standard contract conditions ("small print") are said to be "incorporated by reference" into the contract when it carries such wording at the end of the document as "GAFTA Contract 30 to apply, provided not in contradiction with the above terms", or "provided not in contradiction with the above, the terms of GAFTA 30 are to apply, including its arbitration clauses, all of which the parties admit they have knowledge and notice of, and which they hereby accept".

There is no fixed formula for this clause. The words "the above" refer of course to the particular terms which the parties have agreed to, and which are set out above the incorporation clause. The particular and specific terms agreed to by buyer and seller take precedence legally over the "small print"; the standard language applies, but only if it does not contravene the particular conditions negotiated by the parties. For example, they may have contracted for a transaction f.o.b. vessel stowed and trimmed, and subject to the terms of the NAEGA 2 1982 Contract. The seller is responsible for arranging to perform the stowing and trimming of the grain delivered to the vessel, and for paying the stevedores. This cost is included in the price to the buyer. The specific term overrides the provision of NAEGA 2 calling for delivery to be made "at discharge end of the loading spout". Where there is a contradiction as to terms, the standard conditions must give way. Typewritten language takes precedence over printed material in a contract, on the premise that the parties deliberately elected to depart from the standard provisions. There is a great advantage in being able to include very detailed and lengthy standard conditions by reference, as this permits the bargaining to proceed quickly, with the detailed conditions nonetheless clearly identified.

The importance of standard language may be gauged from a case in

[1] In an advertisement appearing in the trade publication, *Milling and Baking News*, Vol. 61, No. 43, December 21, 1982.

which the official Turkish buying agency purchased 350,000 metric tons of U.S. wheat in 1974 but the letter of credit providing for payment was not opened. The seller obtained favourable original and appeal arbitration awards, as well as subsequent court judgments. It was reported in 1979 that the Turks turned over to the seller 125,000 metric tons of their own wheat in settlement of the court's direction to pay about $80 million in cash.[2] The simple sentence in the contract incorporating the terms of GAFTA 27 and 30 had made possible legal action in England and the adjudication of a very sizeable sum. Had jurisdiction been in Turkey, one might conceive of a different outcome.

Another category of transactions is that between a commercial firm and a governmental agency or official grouping of buyers, usually producers such as millers, feed compounders, etc. Such trades may have much the same legal effect as one involving two commercial firms. The official Portuguese agency Instituto do Azeite e Productos Oleaginosos makes its purchases through brokers. When a government entity makes a purchase of a commercial nature, English and American law holds that it is subject to the same legal rules as a strictly commercial firm. An English judge observed: " . . . a foreign state is entitled to sovereign immunity in respect of its governmental acts but not in respect of its commercial transactions."[3] If the governmental entity agrees to be bound by arbitration, it cannot refuse later to submit to it. Some of the governmental entities which have been parties to London commodity arbitrations, and ensuing litigation in that city, are CHZ Rolimpex (Polish), Agroexport Enterprise for Foreign Trade (Romanian), and Toprak Mahsulleri Ofisi (Turkish). Various other official entities have also participated in arbitrations in London, New York and elsewhere.

The method of purchase of a government entity may be by direct negotiation, called "*gré-à-gré*", such as is done by Exportkhleb, the Russian agency, or by formal, public invitation to submit offers, called "tender" or, in Spanish, "*licitación*". It should be mentioned in passing that while grain people think of "bids" as offers to make a purchase, the word is used in officialese with a broader meaning: offers to buy, sell, or provide a service, as the case may be. In a tender, an announcement is issued stating the date on which offers are to be

[2] *New York Times*, August 16, 1979.

[3] *Planmount Ltd.* v. *The Republic of Zaire* [1980] 2 Lloyd's Rep. 393 (Queen's Bench Division (Commercial Court)).

made, how long they are to remain valid, etc. The tender conditions include the detailed information as to what is to be offered, tonnage and commodity, delivery terms (f.o.b. vessel, c. and f., c.i.f. specified ports or ranges), the delivery period, payment conditions, etc. The announcement may be a lengthy one, running to several pages, or it may consist of a short telex which refers for the small print to standing conditions of a trade association such as GAFTA, or those issued by the buying agency itself. The buyer usually reserves the right to reject all offers, or to accept part of any offer or offers, at its discretion. It is required by various agencies that the offers be accompanied by a "bid bond" or guarantee of fulfilment, for a percentage of the value of the offer, or for a dollar value per ton offered.

The review of the offer may be made in private by the buyer and the participants advised by telephone, followed by a confirming telex, and, in most cases, a formal contract. The Government of Israel Supply Mission in New York works in this way. The offers may have to be presented in the purchaser's country, as in the case of Brazil, Peru, etc. Some purchasers may engage in further negotiations with those having made the offers deemed most favourable to the buyer. The offer with the lowest price is not always *ipso facto* considered to contain the best terms, as there may be other considerations such as quantity offered, delivery periods, etc.

The tender may be a very formal affair, where offers must be presented in sealed envelopes, and are read aloud in public; if they deviate even slightly from the announced conditions, they may be rejected. After the purchases are announced detailed contracts may be issued by the agency, even though the commercial practice is to have the *seller* do this. The transaction is frequently made subject to local law for interpretation and litigation. There is a widespread requirement that sellers must provide the buyer with a performance bond upon being advised that their offer has been accepted. This is usually a guarantee issued by a bank in the form a letter of credit which the buyer may draw against if the seller has not fulfilled its contractual obligations.

U.S. Government regulations require that purchases of grain made under Title I of Public Law 480, be made by open (public) tender held in the United States.

CHAPTER 3

Standard Contract Language

WHO ISSUES STANDARD CONDITIONS?

The GAFTA 30 Contract contains some 276 lines of closely printed, tiny characters: here, "small print" is no mere euphemism! Other standard contracts are also imposing in their length. Who supplies these sets of conditions? The traditional grain contracts world-wide are those of the Grain and Feed Trade Association Ltd., London. This is a trade organisation formed in 1971, amalgamating two earlier groups, the London Corn Trade Association (LCTA) and the Cattle Food Trade Association (Incorporated) (CFTA). GAFTA's forebears give it a distinguished lineage in LCTA, formed in 1878, and in CFTA, established in 1906. By 1888, LCTA had devised some 30 different standard contracts; the number of GAFTA contracts now in force is about 80, covering various grains and feed products, from many origins. "It is estimated that about half of the international trade in grains and a slightly higher proportion of the trade in proteins is carried out on GAFTA contracts or in accordance with their terms."[1]

GAFTA's membership is quite broad, as it includes "producers, shippers, traders, millers, feed merchants, [companies which provide superintending services], arbitrators, and others".[2] A GAFTA report for the year ended September 30, 1981, puts the membership of the Association at 664, drawn from 41 countries.[3]

In addition to formulating contract language and updating it, GAFTA provides the trade with an arbitration mechanism. It also makes available analytical services in support of contract requirements, through three independent laboratories, to which samples are sent from various countries. It also maintains "FAQ" (fair average quality) standards, and runs a futures market in Common Market wheat and barley.

[1] Pamphlet, *GAFTA Today* (London: undated, 1982?).
[2] *Ibid.*
[3] GAFTA: ". . . President's Report . . . Year ended 30th September 1981" (London, 1981), pp. 18–19.

The Association has an important role in trade policy, through its contacts with agencies of the government of the United Kingdom and the European Economic Community. It follows particularly the maze of EEC regulations regarding the Common Agricultural Policy, and currency regulations; and keeps its members informed of these developments. It also works closely with trade groups overseas, and is a highly respected and prestigious organisation.

The year 1971 must have been propitious for amalgamations in London, as it saw not only the formation of GAFTA, but also the formation of the Federation of Oils, Seeds and Fats Associations, known by its acronym "FOSFA". FOSFA's roots are even more venerable than GAFTA's, since it has in its parentage an organisation formed in 1863, the Incorporated Oil & Seeds Association. Its other ancestors are the London Oil & Tallow Trade Association (1910), the London Copra Association (1913), and the Seed, Oil, Cake & General Produce Association (1935). The Association has over 500 members drawn from about 40 countries; they are "producers, shippers, merchants, brokers, crushers, refiners, [companies providing superintending services], laboratories and others involved in various ways in the trade".[4]

FOSFA International, as it is now known, sees its main functions as issuing standard contracts and keeping them current. Emphasis is placed on "establish[ing] greater uniformity in commercial usages, forms of contract and other documents, and the voluntary adoption of such contracts and documents by the trade internationally". The Federation publishes more than 40 contracts and estimates that "85% of the total amount traded internationally" in oilseeds, oils and fats is done under FOSFA contracts. Some of these transactions are "in string", in which a parcel may be bought and sold many times over, but each trade is covered by a contract.

FOSFA International, like GAFTA, holds an important place in commodity arbitrations, maintaining a forum for original actions and for appeal arbitrations.

FOSFA International owns a laboratory which is run as a joint venture with the Food Research Association. Here are analysed the samples which are submitted from all over the world, in accordance with contract provisions, enabling FOSFA International to publish statistics showing the quality ranges, for any given time, of the

[4] This quotation and those in the following paragraph are from a pamphlet, *Introducing . . . FOSFA* (London: undated, 1982?).

products in which its members are interested. The laboratory is also used to carry on research on various matters of interest to the trade. The Federation establishes standards for sampling and analysis, drawing on criteria established by international, specialised agencies; where necessary, new standards are issued by FOSFA International, to satisfy the particular needs of its contracts.

In the same way as GAFTA, its sister organisation, FOSFA International, co-operates with influential trade organisations in countries overseas, with the object of advancing the interests of the trade at large.

The North American Export Grain Association, Inc. ("NAEGA"), is an organisation comprised of some 34 members, private commercial firms and co-operatives domiciled in the United States and Canada. They are buyers and sellers of grain for export, and brokers, NAEGA was incorporated in 1920 and was located in New York until 1976, when it moved to Washington. Its chief objective is to facilitate and promote exports of grain, and its standing committees assist to that end.

NAEGA's Contract Number 1, which I believe was written on c.i.f. terms, has passed into history, as has, more recently, Number 3, for delivery on the West Coast. Form Number 2, f.o.b. vessel for loadings from the United States and Canada, is authoritative and widely accepted. Its Addendum 1, a loading rate guarantee, is precise and meticulous; it has no counterpart in GAFTA or FOSFA.

THE OBJECTIVE OF STANDARD CONTRACT LANGUAGE

What should standard contract language aim to achieve? The foreword to FOSFA International's *Manual*[5] invokes "the ideal of contracts freed from the possibility of misunderstanding and dispute". This is, of course, a tall order, albeit a highly commendable one. No matter how careful the drafters of the small print may be, they will be unable to foresee all the circumstances which may come within the ambit of the terms they are drafting. There is a tradition that a standard contract, which may have been Scandinavian, called for payment "on first presentation of shipping documents", a formula

[5] *FOSFA International Manual* (London, 1981). This is a loose-leaf publication systematically listing all clauses of FOSFA contracts.

designed to protect the legitimate and vital interests of the seller and which seemed to be routine or, in the argot of the trade, "boilerplate", as well as entirely fair. A buyer is said to have rejected shipping documents because of a minor clerical error. The seller made the necessary correction and resubmitted the documents to the buyer, which again rejected them, this time on the ground that, according to the contract, payment was to be made against *first* presentation, whereas this was the second submission of the papers.

The buyer undoubtedly had an eye cocked to the financial benefit to be gained from holding the seller in default. The lure of a profit in cases such as this one, is sometimes irresistible. An arbitration was held to decide the issue, and to the consternation of most of the trade, the buyer was held to have been justified in rejecting the documents. The authors of the standard contract which created this untoward situation cannot be faulted for lack of foresight. The award, however, may be considered an aberration, since panels ordinarily are guided, in interpreting contracts, by what they see as the intent of the parties—or what must have been in their contemplation—at the time of contracting. This approach is more fruitful, and legally correct, than slavish adherence to words taken out of context. The GAFTA contracts, whether or not as a result of this unfortunate experience, have for a long time contained the phrase: "No obviously clerical error in the documents shall entitle the Buyer to reject them or delay payment, but Seller shall be responsible for all loss or expense caused to Buyer by reason of such error, and Seller shall on request of Buyer furnish an approved guarantee in respect thereto."

A more recent problem is that of c.i.f. sales calling for payment against shipping documents presented to seller on arrival of the vessel at the discharge port, but not later than a stipulated time, for example, 20 days after bill of lading date for shipments from the U.S. Gulf of Mexico. The seller extends financing to the buyer until the ship has reached its destination, and presumably has reflected the interest expense in the offering price. If the vessel sinks en route, it is still possible for the seller to collect from the buyer, who will be compensated under the marine insurance coverage. Litigation brought out that this clause could be interpreted to the detriment of a seller who by inadvertence missed the deadline for presentation of the documents. An English Court of Appeal held that: "the sellers failed to tender documents by the time they were obliged to do so under the contracts, and, . . . that this failure entitled the buyers to reject the documents when tendered late."[6] This unintended result was brought about by inadequate contract language. FOSFA 24 rectifies the deficiency: payment is to be made "on or (at Buyer's option) before arrival of the ship at port of destination, but not later than the number of days of [i.e., after] the Bill of Lading as specified hereafter, *unless documents are presented thereafter*". (The number of days are then shown for shipment from four coasts of export.)

Standard contract language should be clear, unambiguous, and brief. These ideals of draftsmanship cannot always be met, as some terms deal with rather involved concepts. A foreign national, whose command of English was not perfect, was nonplussed when he read the GAFTA clause: "The goods are not warranted free from defect, rendering same unmerchantable, which would not be apparent on reasonable examination, any statute or rule of law to the contrary notwithstanding". On first acquaintance, this clause might baffle anyone unfamiliar with legal formulations; such a means of expression is not to be tolerated in contracts unless it is indispensable to satisfy a point of law.

Sometimes the attempt to amend a standard contract so as to remove a flaw or to correct an omission may itself fall short of providing an ideal cure. A judgment by an English law court held that a notice of appropriation given for a c.i.f. contract was invalid. The name of the ship, cited in a telex, had been slightly misspelt, so that it corresponded to another, existing vessel, then located at an enormous distance from the required loading area. The error may have been due to a clerical slip in verifying the spelling in a ships' register. The appropriation had the words "or better name" after the ship's name. The buyer refused to pay for the documents, and was upheld by the court which decided that, under the terms of the contract, an error in the vessel's name would have been open to correction had it been made strictly in the process of transmission of the message. In the circumstances, however, the seller could not amend the name of the vessel, and the appropriation was invalid.[7] Faced with this judicial decision, GAFTA and FOSFA both devised a new phrase to be incorporated into their contracts, and each came up with an entirely different formula. FOSFA put it in a short and direct way: "Any

[6] *Topefer* v. *Lenersan-Poortman N.V.—Toepfer* v. *Verheijdens Vervoeder Commissiehandel* [1980] 1 Lloyd's Rep. 148.

[7] *Kleinjan & Holst N.V.* v. *Bremer Handelsgesellschaft m.b.H.* [1972] 2 Lloyd's Rep. 11.

slight variation in the ship's name shall not invalidate the declaration." GAFTA, on the other hand, produced this more exotic version: "An appropriation shall not be deemed invalid if the date of Bill of Lading is within the contract period and if on that date the vessel named is at the port of loading and carrying goods of the contractual description and quantity." Anyone not familiar with the story behind this last clause might be excused for not being able to discern its objective.

THE SCOPE OF STANDARD CONTRACTS

What should be the scope of standard contracts? They should set out the rules for those things which are inherent to the transaction and vital to its fulfilment. The rules cannot, obviously, cover all contingencies which may come up in the execution of a grain contract. For example, there is no provision in GAFTA 30 to cover the instance of a payment made by a buyer to a bank which becomes bankrupt before passing the payment along to the seller. In a rather complex case of this nature, a court held that the seller was to be reimbursed by the buyer, despite the fact that the latter had already effected payment to the bank.[8]

GAFTA and FOSFA contracts have nothing to say about the rights and obligations of the parties in the event that a performing vessel sinks before payment is made. The question might hinge largely on whether a notice of appropriation had been given before the casualty took place.

Likewise, NAEGA 2 is silent on the seller's duties if a loading elevator is incapacitated by an explosion, which the seller claims makes it impossible to effect delivery. The resolution of this question would probably depend on the provisions of the Uniform Commercial Code, taking account of all the relevant circumstances.

It is interesting to note that in GAFTA 27 and 30, FOSFA 24, and NAEGA 2 (all of which deal with exports from the United States and Canada), the words *force majeure* do not appear, although various elements of this legal concept are covered in some detail in the contracts, for instance, strikes, prohibition of exports and acts of government. The expression *Act of God* is also absent, yet one might

[8] *E.D. & F. Man Ltd.* v. *Nigerian Sweets & Confectionery Co., Ltd.* [1977] 2 Lloyd's Rep. 50.

surmise that a tornado crippling a loading facility would, in certain circumstances, provide some relief to the seller in its contractual obligations.

Standard language was never intended to cover all of the extraordinary and unexpected things which can happen in the performance of a contract or all aspects of a foreseeable occurrence. The contracts are quite lengthy enough as they are; in addition, the cause of fairness is not served by convoluted and rigid rules. When problems of an unusual nature arise which cannot be resolved by the parties themselves, the best solution is referral to trade usage and to arbitration, rather than trying to devise very complex rules which would not be suitable for all occurrences. An arbitration panel is in an ideal position to sift through all the facts, and to arrive at an award which applies the relevant law to those facts.

There is no doubt that standard contracts have greatly contributed to the orderly working-out of transactions. When the rules are fair, correspond to commercial reality, and are clearly stated, the number of disputes is kept to a minimum. The standard contracts issued by trade organisations, widely used and well understood, are complemented and elucidated by trade custom. Further insight may be gained from arbitration awards and, particularly in England, from litigation. It is hard to imagine how the trade could carry on efficiently without the convenience of standard rules, tested over the years and kept current.

KEEPING STANDARD CONTRACTS UP TO DATE

The standard contracts should codify the usages of the trade, and when these change, the contracts should be amended.

Unfortunately, the grain trade must be enamoured of its past, judging by the reluctance with which it faces the task of making changes. When made quickly, they are usually the product of a dire occurrence, such as the 1973 U.S. embargo on soyabeans, soyabean meal, and other commodities. If the need to amend is not obvious, members of the trade may feel that deviations from long-standing clauses may somehow jeopardise their existing contracts.

It is bemusing to note that the GAFTA 30 Contract retains, under the heading "QUALITY", this clause: "On sales of Canadian produce

Seller shall have the option of delivering the Official Canadian Inspection Certificate issued in the United States." Canadian grain was transhipped regularly through the United States to Europe and elsewhere, but this movement ceased decades ago, and the flow of exports has been reversed, with sizeable quantities of U.S. grain being exported through the Canadian St Lawrence. Yet the clause has subsisted despite revision of the contract.

It took several years after loading guarantees had become a regular feature of f.o.b. vessel contracts in the United States before NAEGA 2's Addendum 1 was issued. In extenuation, however, it may be argued that by that time there had been enough experience with the concept to make it possible to identify most of the problems, and thus to draft thoughtful and comprehensive clauses.

Despite what we have said, the trade organisations do eventually amend their contracts when necessity dictates it, and when a working consensus is reached. The reluctance to use new language is witness not only to the conservative approach of individual members of the trade, but also to the fact that they feel free to bargain on terms other than those of the standard contracts. Even though the NAEGA 2 form was completely revised in 1978 and reissued with minor modifications in 1982, some soyabeans contracts continue to be made on the terms of the *1973* NAEGA 2 contract. Slips are issued for amendments made to the standard contracts by the associations, avoiding an immediate reissue of the entire document. Slips are also used for certain optional clauses which the parties agree upon. Amendments are announced in the GAFTA and FOSFA monthly newsletters.

Changes in the various aspects of the grain business have been dramatic over the years. The book of London Corn Trade Association (LCTA) contracts, issued in 1922, lists some 73 forms, each as large as those in use today, and with the print just as infinitesimal. As late as 1931, the list in LCTA's book included no less than four contracts for shipment by sailing vessel!

Forgotten are those great adventures known as the grain races, which can still be savoured in a book called *The Last Grain Race*.[9] The participants in the contests were sailing vessels bringing grain from Australia to Western Europe. These were not races in the sense that the ships all departed from the same port at the same time, but they engaged the spirit and imagination of the seamen and others

[9] Eric Newby, *The Last Grain Race* (London: Secker & Warburg, 1956).

fascinated by their exploits. The last of the grain races was held in 1939, and we are told that the winner was the vessel *Moshulu*, which took 82 days outbound from Belfast to Port Lincoln, Australia. The return voyage, carrying 59,000 bags, or 4,875 tons of wheat, kept the vessel at sea 91 days, from Port Victoria to Queenstown, Ireland. These voyages were made by a tough breed of men who went to sea for small wages, doing rigorous and perilous work. Passage around Cape Horn was particularly hazardous, and it was not at all rare for vessels to be lost in the frenzied gales which felled masts and tore rigging apart.

The "Liberty" and similar types of vessels built during the Second World War were used for many years thereafter in ocean transportation. They had a uniform carrying capacity of some 9,500 long tons, 5% more or less. The contractual provision of loading tolerance "at vessel's option" meant that, since the deviation in quantity loaded to the vessel from 9,500 long tons would be attributable to the requirements of proper stowage, and not the particular interests of the buyer or seller, the tolerance would in effect be determined by the master, or "at vessel's option". The deviation (within 5% more or less), would be invoiced at contract price. The expression "at vessel's option" has little meaning today, as ships differ enormously in carrying capacity.

The vessels which roam the seas at present provide quite a contrast with the sailing vessels of yesteryear. Bulk carriers, of course, accomplish their voyage in a much shorter time than the older ships. They are "self-trimming", and their carrying capacity is 30,000 tons of bulk grain and more, sometimes considerably more. There is no intention to operate these vessels at a leisurely pace; any time lost at anchorage waiting to load or to discharge cargo prevents the vessel from proceeding on another voyage, which presumably is its main source of income. Thus, demurrage/dispatch clauses encourage the suppliers of the cargo at loading, and the receivers at discharge, to operate promptly so as to release the vessel, thus enabling it to be on its way once again. Loading and discharge rate guarantees are now a regular feature not only of charter-parties, but also of grain contracts, whether f.o.b. vessel or c. and f. or c.i.f.

The speed of loading and discharging may be an objective of the vessel owners; it is just as important to owners of efficient loading and discharging facilities. Grain elevators are huge structures, capable of handling large amounts of grain per hour. Speed of operations for optimum use of the facility is as much their concern as it is that of the vessel owners. The most modern facility on the Mississippi River expects, upon completion of remodelling, to have a loading-out capacity of some 4,500 tons per hour! Unit trains of hopper-cars greatly facilitate the speedy flow of grain to the seaboard.

As we have indicated, NAEGA's Addendum 1 sets out the rules for the calculation of demurrage/despatch at loading for f.o.b. vessel contracts. GAFTA 64, the f.o.b. vessel contract, and the c.i.f. contracts GAFTA 27 and 30 and FOSFA 24 do not codify terms of loading and discharge guarantees. One reason may be that these conditions are difficult to standardise when dealing with so many possible origins and destinations.

Another fundamental shift in the trade has been the adoption by buyers in many parts of the world of the method of purchasing "on the basis" ("*prix-à-fixer*"), i.e., at an agreed "basis" or "premium" price over or under (or at) the price of a futures contract. When the futures are exchanged, the "flat" price is fixed. This pricing mechanism has long been in use in the U.S.; the NAEGA 2 contract of 1973 referred to it, and it is dealt with in greater length in the 1978 and 1982 versions. There is, however, no mention of it in GAFTA 64, or GAFTA 27 or 30, or FOSFA 24.

There have, of course, been many changes affecting the business. One of them is the result of concern about the soundness of the commodity to be delivered. Russian and Chinese contracts contain long lists of prohibitions or limitations as to pathogens, residues of pesticides, etc. Since each destination has its own standards for these items, they have to be dealt with on a country-by-country basis. It seems that every couple of years or so a particular problem has to be resolved with respect to the condition of the crop: corn blight, excessive ergot, sprout damage, wheat scab, etc. Solutions are usually found through the efforts of the exporting community, importing countries, and the authorities of each, if necessary.

When a trade organisation goes out of existence without leaving a successor, exceptional care should be taken in contracting on standard terms which become obsolete without the possibility of amendments. Every now and again courts are obliged to nominate arbitrators because charter-parties carry the New York Produce Exchange arbitration clause. This august Exchange gave up its commodity and freight functions some ten years ago.

THE PALM-OIL POOL CONTRACT "CAPER"

We have emphasised the importance of the standard conditions, the small print which governs the purchase and sale of commodities. In the Palm-Oil Pool Contract "Caper", any number of transactions were religiously made subject to a standard form. The trade, however, cared little about its contents. Trading in palm-oil was a game played under the delusion that a set of rules applied, which was unknown to the participants, and, worse yet, which had never even seen the light of day! This curious act of blind faith on the part of so many ostensibly hard-headed traders lasted no less than two years.

The steep growth in production of Far Eastern palm-oil in the late 1960s proved quite a boon to international commerce: brokers and traders on three continents launched themselves into this business, with perhaps more alacrity than good judgment. Strings of half a dozen parties, and often many more, aroused no concern; everyone was confident of making money, despite the risks of trading in a flat price commodity, with no effective futures market. In fact, the large number of transactions seemed to provide some assurance of market breadth and liquidity. When all the illusions had dissipated, this South-Sea Bubble burst, and only the brokers came away unscathed.

In the frenetic rush to trade, little heed was given to "details of execution", which were too pedestrian and mundane for most traders. Somehow, before long, all c.i.f. contracts were being made subject to the general terms of a standard contract called Malaysian Palmoil Pool Contract ("MPOP"). Often, there was an option to deliver Sumatra palm-oil, subject to the terms of a contract issued by the Netherlands Oils, Fats and Oilseeds Trade Association ("NOFOTA"). The rules of NOFOTA were well known and its arbitration mechanism was effective. An inquisitive contract specialist sought a copy of the MPOP Contract for his files, in case questions of interpretation should come up, but traders were somewhat contemptuous: while "money is being made by all", the question of standard terms seems tiresome and irrelevant. This failed to satisfy the punctilious technician who pursued the search vigorously, eventually directing inquiries to Rotterdam and to Malaysia. Everyone was certain that the contract existed, but no one seemed to have a copy of it. It appeared that a Rotterdam broker had deposited a copy of the alleged MPOP Contract with the local Chamber of Commerce, or similar body, in keeping with the custom of that market. Upon examination, it was found that the contract was not the genuine, elusive, MPOP, but one drafted by the broker. The answer finally came from Malaysia, and it was similarly discouraging. The fact had to be faced: there simply was no MPOP Contract, but only one drawn up by a large producer, Felda Land Development Company. This document was not at all suitable for trading the commodity in world markets, still, myriads of transactions continued to be made subject to the evanescent contract styled "MPOP". Only the technician was distressed, and all the brokers and scores of trading companies still seemed unconcerned.

One day, inevitably, a dispute came up on a shipment of Malaysian palm-oil. The issue could no longer be evaded: what trading rules applied? The claimant simply selected FOSFA, whose rules and arbitration are widely accepted in the vegetable oils business. Happily, the dispute involved a question which all relevant FOSFA contracts treated in the same manner; otherwise there could have been a further controversy as to which of the FOSFA standard contracts should be used. Luckily for the claimant, the respondent did not challenge the choice of forum or rules, but this was a close call. Had the respondent stood its ground, the dispute could have dragged on for years in courts of law, with even the possibility of legal argument over the country in which the proceedings should take place.

Then another disagreement arose over a contract for Malaysian and/or Sumatran palm-oil, where the choice of origin was up to the seller. The seller had not declared any intention, and was not required to do so until shipment was made. Should the arbitration, if one could legally be demanded, proceed before FOSFA or before NOFOTA? In each case, the respondent might claim that proper jurisdiction belonged in the other forum! These problems could only be overcome if both parties were in good faith and did not interpose objections to a reasonable choice of forum. What risks were needlessly undertaken by so many trading firms!

It gradually dawned on the players in the game that they had neglected their vital interests by rashly assuming the existence of a standard contract which turned out to be a delusion. They had just shrugged the problem away when it was brought to their attention. That so many of them fell into such a grievous error is only mildly surprising, given their disdain for what they considered mere "paperwork". Yet they would certainly not have thought of accepting an insurance policy for a large amount of coverage without the small print being there in all its mind-boggling detail.

With the occasional appearance of problems in execution and of impending insolvencies, the trade finally started to make its contracts subject to the rules and the arbitration of the National Institute of Oilseed Products ("NIOP"). These were by no means perfect, but they did save the trade from the indignity of continuously making deals subject to imaginary rules.

In 1973 FOSFA issued Contract No. 80, for crude unbleached palm-oil in bulk, delivered weights. This was the joint work of FOSFA and the Malaysian Palm Oil Producers' Association, Kuala Lumpur. By now many traders and even some brokers had abandoned palm-oil and had gone on to other activities. There were several major bankrupticies in Malaysia and elsewhere, with wide "ripple effects", as the oil was customarily sold in large strings of transactions, and many firms were adversely affected. The strings were so frequent and extensive that in one notorious case arbitrators spun together in one string no less than 49 contracts, in which most parties made more than one appearance. In some cases, parties winning arbitrations were still trying to get awards enforced many years later, yet they may have been luckier than those who had unsatisfied debts from firms that had gone bankrupt!

The tale of the MPOP Contract is almost humorous in showing how realistic merchants who are used to exercising prudent business judgment surrender critical acumen, rather than deal with "technicalities". It should be added, though, that today it is doubtful that we would see a repeat of the MPOP Contract case, as greater sophistication prevails and closer attention is paid to contractual matters.

CHAPTER 4

The Major Contract Provisions

F.O.B. VESSEL, C. AND F. AND C.I.F. CONTRACT TERMS

What is the importance of the distinction between the three major types of sales terms in the export grain business, i.e., free on board ("f.o.b.") vessel, cost and freight ("c. and f."), and cost, insurance and freight ("c.i.f.")? These terms establish the buyer's and the seller's rights and duties, they define legal relationships between them, and they present the parties with trading risks and opportunities.

F.o.b. vessel sales

Under this type of transaction, the seller is obliged to have grain meeting contract specifications available at the export loading facility ready for delivery to the vessel at the time or times required by the contract, and to effect this loading. It is the buyer's duty to provide a vessel ready to accept delivery at the proper time and, certainly not least, to pay for the shipping documents representing the grain delivered. From these broad obligations arise others: the buyer must nominate the vessel in sufficient time to allow the seller to make arrangements for delivery. The contract calls for a pre-advice period, usually a minimum of 10 days, between the date of the vessel nomination and the date on which the seller assumes any obligation to effect delivery. If the specific loading port and elevator are not named in the contract, the seller must designate them. There are many other features to grain contracts, sometimes involving complications which keep specialists gainfully employed.

NAEGA 2 calls for delivery to be accomplished at the end of the loading spout. Grain is drawn from an elevator's bins, elevated, weighed in hopper scales, and dropped into the vessel's holds through a pipe called a "spout". "Delivery at the end of the loading spout" signifies that risk of loss passes to the buyer at that point.

Clause 25 of NAEGA 2 provides that the seller retains title to the goods loaded until payment in full has been received. If a ship which has picked up the cargo sinks alongside the loading elevator, the seller has nonetheless accomplished its task and is entitled to payment against presentation of the required shipping documents. The buyer, responsible for placing marine insurance, will make payment to the seller and lodge a claim against the underwriter for reimbursement of its outlay or possibly for the replacement value of the lost cargo.

C. and f. and c.i.f. sales

Cost and freight transactions oblige the seller to supply the commodity satisfying the contract specifications, loaded on a vessel provided by the seller, at the time or times stipulated in the contract. The seller must make all arrangements necessary to have the grain in the loading position. The seller must also supply the vessel, usually by entering into a voyage or time charter-party, in which the seller acts as the charterer, and contracts to use a vessel for a particular voyage, or for a period of time, with the vessel owner supplying bunkers, crew and the necessaries for the transportation and loading and discharge of grain. The c. and f./c.i.f. seller does not *guarantee* the actual arrival of the vessel at the port of destination. If the vessel is disabled en route, but the seller has fulfilled all its obligations, including appropriating the goods in timely fashion, the seller is entitled to payment, and the buyer's recourse is with the vessel owner and/or the insurance underwriter. The charter-party is an undertaking separate from the contract of sale for the grain, although in some of their terms, e.g., commodity, ports of loading and discharge, and dates of performance, these two agreements must be identical or compatible.

C. and f. contracts require the buyer to cover the marine insurance, while c.i.f. contracts place this duty on the seller.

C. and f. and c.i.f. terms are virtually identical, therefore we discuss them as a unit in this book. Similarly, GAFTA 27 and 30 and FOSFA 24, although strictly speaking c.i.f. contracts, are also used for c. and f. trades, and we refer to them as a single concept.

C. and f. and c.i.f. contracts involve greater risks and greater opportunities for the seller, than do f.o.b. vessel transactions. To the risks of merchandising and delivering the commodity are added those of booking and performing ocean freight undertakings.

The most obvious opportunity for the c. and f. and c.i.f. seller is that it can "take a position" in ocean freight based on the belief that the rates will rise or fall. This chance to make a profit, however, involves a concomitant risk of loss.

The logistics of c. and f. and c.i.f. sales are more favourable to the seller than those of f.o.b. vessel sales. In the latter, the two chief elements, i.e., the commodity and the freight, are controlled, the first by the seller, and the second by the buyer. If a transaction is made with a one-month delivery period, the seller will not know beforehand when within the month the grain will be loaded, until a vessel nomination is received from the buyer. In c. and f./c.i.f. trades, however, the seller may charter ocean freight for a given period within the month. One can readily see that with both elements in hand, barge or rail demurrage may be reduced, grain may perhaps be purchased with more favourable timing, etc. Making c. and f./c.i.f. sales of parcels (less than full cargo quantities) to active markets enables one to accumulate, in time, transactions in quantities sufficient to charter an entire vessel, at a freight rate presumably lower than that used when calculating the sale prices for the parcels.

Imposing sums of money have been lost in c. and f./c.i.f. sales because of the seller's inability to collect demurrage at discharge from the buyer. Vessels have had to wait for extended periods at the port of destination because no berth was available, and because discharge operations were very time-consuming. In some instances, it has been extremely difficult, if not impossible, to collect large sums due. The seller expecting problems of this kind is well advised to trade on f.o.b. vessel terms, or to cushion the sale price with a margin corresponding to the estimated demurrage.

What determines the delivery basis to govern a transaction? Most importing countries or individual buyers have a preference for one of the three, because of local laws, established custom, commercial keenness, knowledge of the freight markets, etc. The seller generally has little influence over the choice, except of course in the rare cases where offers are requested both f.o.b. vessel and c. and f./c.i.f. The seller may feel that the c. and f./c.i.f. terms afford it an advantage sufficient to enable it to discount these prices, as against f.o.b. vessel offers.

With the vertical integration of the business on the Continent, specialised firms have assumed the functions involved in purchasing grain f.o.b. vessel at origin and delivering it to interior mills or processing plants, e.g., on the River Rhine. These companies are skilful in trading cash grain, futures, ocean freight, foreign exchange, and (when permitted by Common Market rules), import levies. "Delivered" markets are very competitive, so that the real gains are made by the industrial buyers, which make cheap purchases and avoid risks.

The standard contracts do not systematically list the elements of the three types of delivery, though they touch on some points; others are passed over. Nothing is said about which party must obtain and pay for shipping documents such as weight and inspection certificates. Neither is the question broached as what bank charges, if any, the seller must absorb for a letter of credit opened in its favour. There is no reference in our c. and f./c.i.f. contracts to the buyer's obligation—if any—to obtain an import licence. Filling in these gaps is not very difficult. Shipping documents are, by long-established custom, obtained and paid for by the seller, as being best able to make the necessary arrangement at the loading port. Bank charges are for account of the buyer, in the absence, of course, of an understanding to the contrary. Incoterms specify that, for c. and f./c.i.f. transactions, the buyer must procure and provide, at its own risk and expense, any import licence or permit or the like which may be required for importation of the goods at destination.

Incoterms, issued by the International Chamber of Commerce, are an official catalogue of the obligations of buyer and seller under various types of contractual deliveries, including those discussed here. A similar glossary is the American Foreign Trade Definitions. This appears to have been largely supplanted by the Incoterms, which themselves are rarely referred to in the grain trade.

THE USE OF STANDARD CONTRACT LANGUAGE

It should be emphasised that parties may choose any lawful conditions which they mutually agree upon. Trade organisations do no more than supply convenient and, one hopes, well thought-out clauses, but there is no obligation whatever on the part of their members or others to use these terms. Buyer and seller may hammer out in detail each and every one of the conditions they wish to be bound by. The parties may agree on a standard contract with modifications of their own, or they may prefer to make a "cocktail" of clauses from different standard rules. "Centro terms" and "ANEC terms", respectively, for commodities of Argentine and Brazilian origins, make use of standard GAFTA conditions, in addition to their own clauses. C. and f. sales of feed grains to Japan are made under the terms of JF–1, a set of rules formulated by a Japanese trade group, chiefly for ocean transportation; they incorporate GAFTA 27 and 30 by reference. Trade associations on the European Continent have developed their own clauses, used in conjunction with the GAFTA and FOSFA terms.

If standard terms are to apply, they should be those best suited to the particular transaction, and this may take a little study. Although GAFTA 64 and NAEGA 2 are both f.o.b. vessel contracts, they are quite dissimilar in their treatment of loading tolerances and loading obligations, to cite only two examples. GAFTA 64 provides for an extension of delivery if requested by the buyer. English law, which governs, permits the seller to stop loading the vessel upon the expiration of the delivery period, or of the extension period. This can be disastrous when a vessel arrives shortly before the end of the delivery period (or the extended delivery period), as the buyer may find itself with its ship partially loaded, and the seller unwilling to put one more bushel of grain on board! NAEGA 2, on the other hand, would oblige the seller to complete the delivery, in the absence, of course, of extraordinary circumstances.

NAMES OF BUYERS, SELLERS AND BROKERS

It is important not only that the full and correct name of buyer and seller be given in the contract, but also their current addresses. These days, firms are apt to have offices, branches, affiliates or other appendages here or there. Without proper care, notices may be transmitted to the wrong office, which may think itself justified in simply ignoring them. As a result, notices may be considered as not having been sent by the required deadlines, with serious consequences. In an ingenious attempt to overcome the "time barrier", a firm gave a vessel nomination by telexing it to the West Coast office of the seller. The contract was with the seller's East Coast office, but an imaginative fellow in the buyer's employ thought that a telex sent at 6 p.m. New York time would be a splendid way to meet the deadline for notices, with the clocks on Pacific time showing 3 p.m. Since the seller named in the contract was clearly located in New York, the ploy did not work.

From another standpoint, the name of one's counterpart is the most important item in the contract: it is vital to "know whom one is dealing with", both in a literal and figurative sense, as the integrity of the contract depends on the honesty and capacity of the parties to fulfil it.

A buyer of a f.o.b. vessel cargo was having second thoughts about lifting the grain, as market prices had dropped considerably and, rather than follow Lincoln's precept that a bad bargain should be hugged the tighter, devised a cunning scheme. The seller was asked to have the contract redrawn naming another firm as purchaser, whose faithful performance would be guaranteed by the original buyer. The new contract was submitted by the seller, but it was never countersigned; the guarantee was, however, executed and delivered to the seller. It turned out that the second buyer was a company owned, at least in part, by the original one. No vessel nomination was forthcoming: the seller demanded satisfaction from the guarantor, and was rebuffed. The disingenuous argument went that the original contract was no longer valid, having been displaced by the second one, with the guarantee. The second contract had no legal effect, not having been countersigned, and the guarantee for this transaction was equally a dead letter. Despite the remarkably inventive nature of the argument, the arbitrators were not impressed, and awarded in favour of the seller. Other accounts of this kind can be given; they all point to the fact that knowing with whom one is dealing may often be much more important than putting together a deal which looks very profitable, and founders because of a breach or an insolvency.

As notices may be given through a broker, the latter should be clearly named in the contract. There is a curious difference in the phrasing of this provision, between GAFTA and FOSFA contracts. GAFTA 27 and 30 both read: "A Notice to the Broker or Agent shall be deemed a Notice under this contract." FOSFA says: "Notice from a broker shall be a valid notice under this contract." GAFTA talks about the notice being given *to* the broker or agent, while FOSFA, about its being received *from* the broker. The matter might be of more than academic interest if the message is not passed on or is delayed in transmission by the broker. Does the GAFTA rule relieve the sender of liability once the notice has been properly given to the broker? Does the FOSFA clause mean that the notice is not effectively made, unless it is actually passed on to the addressee? The GAFTA text also permits the advices to be made, for instance, by the American affiliate of a buyer or seller in Europe, but this agent must presumably be named in the contract.

QUANTITY

Sales of U.S. and Canadian grain are usually made for the delivery of a quantity stated in metric tons, and at a price stated per metric ton, e.g., "25,000 metric tons, 5% more or less, of U.S. No. 3 or better Yellow Corn, at U.S. $150.00 per metric ton f.o.b. vessel U.S. Gulf". A question which often baffles newcomers to the trade is, why must the contract specify a conversion ratio between the U.S. system of weights and the metric system? To determine the quantity actually loaded, one must, of course, physically weigh the commodity. Scales in the United States are, by law, still calibrated in pounds, although Canadian exports are weighed in kilos.

Say the scales for a loading in the United States give a reading of 57,322,835 lbs. This amount must be converted into metric tons, to ascertain whether the contract quantity was loaded (viz., between 23,750 and 26,250 metric tons), and in order to arrive at the invoice value. GAFTA, FOSFA and NAEGA 2 contracts specify a conversion ratio of 2,240 lbs. = 1,016 kilos (or 1.016 metric tons). Thus,

$$\frac{57{,}322{,}835 \times 1{,}016}{2{,}240}$$

or 26,000 metric tons. It should be explained that the trade lives with a number of conversion ratios. For example, there are several kinds of tons in use; the traditional one in the maritime domain was the long ton of 2,240 lbs., which appears in our conversion rate to the metric ton. The nearly universal acceptance of the metric system will sooner or later move the U.S., however reluctantly, from pro-forma to actual adoption of the metric system. In the 1970s, Great Britain took a formal step in this direction, prompting a French grain man to send his London colleagues a good-natured gibe: "Welcome to the XVIIIth Century!"

The metric ton is always composed of 1,000 kilos, just as the foot is always made up of 12 inches, and should not be confused with the 1,016 kilos, which is strictly an element in the conversion ratio between the American and the metric systems. By the way, the metric ton is sometimes referred to in the United States and Great Britain as a "tonne", which distinguishes it from the long ton, the short ton, etc., at least when written. Until a new pronunciation is devised, this worthy attempt at lucidity will be of limited help in conversations.

The conversion factor from the U.S. system to the metric is necessary also when the quantity sold is expressed in American units (e.g., long tons of 2,240 lbs. each), with the price stated per metric ton.

The trade in the United States regularly uses the bushel as a unit of weight. Originally, the bushel basket was a unit of volume, and the weight of a bushel would vary according to the specific gravity of its contents. The bushel is a handy reference for those who operate elevators, and/or ship grain by rail, truck, etc. The number of pounds assigned to a bushel of a given commodity is fixed, and the bushel has become a unit of weight for each commodity. Thus for purposes of conversion, a bushel of corn always stands for a weight of 56 lbs. A bushel of barley, a lighter commodity, is fixed at 48 lbs. Whether one talks of 50,000 bushels of corn or 50,000 bushels of barley, the volume of each should tend to be the same, so that the space taken up in an elevator by 50,000 bushels of corn would *approximate* to that taken up by 50,000 bushels of barley. We say "approximate" because the *actual* test weight (or specific gravity) of the commodity will not be equal to that fixed as the constant of weight. The bushel is important in international trade of U.S. grain, as an increasing number of sales are made with price to be fixed, i.e., at a basis over, under or at, the value of a futures contract, with prices expressed per bushel of grain.

How much the grain weighs when loaded into an ocean vessel must be known to determine whether the contract's quantity requirements are being satisfied, and also in order to invoice the goods. The contract may call for the settlement to be made strictly on the basis of the quantity loaded (styled "bill of lading weight final"), or, in c. and f./c.i.f. sales, there may be a provisional payment based on the loaded weight, and a final accounting later, calculated on the weight as determined at discharge of the goods from the ocean vessel. "Full outturn guarantee", or "delivered weights" refer to settlement on landed weights and require the seller to assume the risk of "normal" loss in weight suffered during the ocean transportation of the commodity. This risk is not covered by marine insurance, but rather by superintendence firms, which charge a premium for the coverage;

the seller may, of course, choose to be self-insured. "Full outturn guarantees" are not a feature of f.o.b. vessel contracts, and they are not always incorporated in c. and f./c.i.f. contracts.

LOADING TOLERANCES

The loading tolerances appearing in our favourite contracts, GAFTA 27 and 30, FOSFA 24 and NAEGA 2, are the creature of ocean freight practices. The contracts involve transportation by sea, and vessels are usually chartered to carry a quantity with a loading tolerance, e.g., 30,000 metric tons, 5% more or less. The tolerance is required because one cannot be certain beforehand of the exact quantity of cargo which a vessel will lift; this will depend on many factors, such as the particular commodity and its "cubic", the requirements of safe stowage, etc. The master of a vessel endeavours to lift as much cargo as possible within the stipulations of a voyage charter, taking account of requirements of safe stowage and navigation, commitments as to the draught of the vessel, etc. The voyage charterer is bound to deliver to the vessel a quantity within the agreed tolerance, except in lump sum agreements. Inevitably, maritime usage came to be adopted in grain contracts which also provide for a margin in the quantity to be delivered. These contracts vary as to the following points:

1. Is the tolerance at the option of the buyer or the seller?
2. What is the percentage of tolerance allowed?
3. How is the quantity over or under the mean contract amount to be priced?
4. How is the tolerance to be treated in the event of partial deliveries?
5. How is the tolerance to be treated in the event of default on the contract?

GAFTA 27 and 30, and FOSFA 24, the c.i.f. contracts, allow the *seller* the right to exercise the tolerance, and NAEGA 2, the f.o.b. vessel contract, gives this right to the *buyer*. These are logical measures, as they leave the option of the tolerance with the presumed charterer of the vessel, corresponding, at least in theory, to the requirements of the charter-party. The f.o.b. vessel purchaser may be able to lift a fixed quantity against a contract, for example, if its lot is the first loaded into the vessel which then loads commodities against other sales. Under NAEGA 2, however, this would be a dubious advantage as the tolerance is priced at the market. Tolerances are sometimes included in large or unusual contracts, to accommodate the needs of the parties and bear little or no relation to stowage requirements.

As we have stated elsewhere, the NAEGA 2 contracts prior to 1978 made the tolerance "at vessel's option"; this approach has become obsolete.

GAFTA 27, the full cargo contract, provides for a total loading tolerance of 10% more or less, GAFTA 30 and FOSFA 24, a total of 5% more less, and NAEGA 2, 5% more or less.

GAFTA 27's clause allows the seller to deliver up to 5% over or under the mean contract amount, with such deviation to be invoiced at the contract price, and an additional 5% more or less on the mean contract amount, to be invoiced at the market price on the last bill of lading date. GAFTA 30 has a similar provision, but the percentages are 2% and 3%, respectively. FOSFA 24's clause is similar to GAFTA 30. NAEGA allows the buyer a tolerance of 5% more or less, all at market price. GAFTA 64, a f.o.b. vessel contract, provides for 5% more or less at contract price, and, in the case of full cargoes, an additional 5% at market price on bill of lading date.

NAEGA 2 takes cognisance of sales "on the basis", and its tolerance clause calls for an additional exchange of futures if the quantity loaded differs by more than 5,000 bushels from the amount of futures previously exchanged; the contract premium is also adjusted to the market.

The contracts mentioned state that the price shall be fixed by arbitration if the parties cannot agree on a figure.

As to the treatment of the tolerance in contracts allowing partial shipments, GAFTA 30 reads: "In the event of more than one delivery being made each delivery shall be considered a separate contract, but the margin on the mean quantity sold shall not be affected thereby." GAFTA 64 has similar wording, viz., that the full amount of the tolerance may be exercised at the time of the last delivery. NAEGA 2 provides that the tolerance is applicable to the unshipped balance only. Assuming a contract for 25,000 metric tons 5% more or less, and a delivery of 10,000 metric tons, there remain to be delivered 15,000 metric tons, with the tolerance of 5% applying only on these 15,000 tons, thus, a quantity between 14,250 and 15,750 metric tons.

GAFTA 27 and 30 and NAEGA 2 are silent as to the quantity on which damages are to be reckoned in the event of a default. FOSFA 24 reads, under the heading of "Default": "Damages to be computed on the mean contract quantity."

GAFTA 119, a f.o.b. vessel contract used for the sale of soyabean meal from the United States, calls for the damages in the event of "default of delivery" to be calculated on the quantity called, or on the mean contract amount. In a case decided by the House of Lords, it was held that the minimum quantity should be used (i.e., the mean quantity less the loading tolerance). This case involved non-delivery of goods by the seller, which alleged that the buyer had not given the vessel nomination within the stipulated deadline. The Lords ruled that the seller had been justified in withholding delivery; since this was a case of "non-performance without breach" by the seller, the damages were to be reckoned on the minimum quantity.[1]

It bears repeating that loading tolerances of any kind may be negotiated between the parties. They may agree, for instance, that a c.i.f. sale shall be for an amount between 20,000 metric tons, 5% more or less, and 23,000 metric tons, 5% more or less, "to be declared upon chartering". Upon chartering, the seller might designate 21,000 metric tons 5% more or less. Buyer and seller contract for tolerances in various ways, which they feel appropriate to the particular circumstances of their transaction.

QUALITY AND CONDITION

There are three major ways to determine the quality of grain, oilseeds and meals, when these are sold in world markets.

1. The commodity may be referred in the contract with a "shorthand" or "grade" designation such as "U.S. No. 2 Hard Red Winter Wheat", or "No. 1 Canada Western Red Spring Wheat". Both the United States and Canada have official standards defining each "grade". U.S. grain, soyabeans and flaxseed sold for export with a grade designation must be officially sampled and analysed ("graded") by, or under the supervision of, the Federal Grain Inspection Service (FGIS), a U.S. Government agency. The Canadian counterpart to the

[1] *Bunge Corporation* v. *Tradax Export S.A.* [1981] 2 Lloyd's Rep. 1. See also *Toprak Mahsulleri Ofisi* v. *Finagrain Compagnie Commerciale Agricole et Financiere, S.A.* [1979] 2 Lloyd's Rep. 98, where the House of Lords awarded damages on maximum amount of contract. The buyer had defaulted, and on the balance of probabilities, the seller would have delivered the maximum quantity.

FGIS is the Canadian Grain Commission. Standards are issued by both agencies, showing the minimum factors making up each grade: test weight, moisture, damage, foreign material, etc.; these factors differ as between commodities and sub-classes. The Canadian standards are amended annually, as the characteristics of the crop may warrant.

In the United States, the inspection may be appealed, which may result in the grade being changed, superseding the original certificate. There is a further opportunity of referral to a Board of Appeals. The official "Grain Standards" cover not only grain, but also two of the oilseeds, soyabeans and flaxseed. The FGIS carries out or supervises the weighing and inspection of grain at ports of shipments. The diverter-type mechanical sampler is used; it cuts across the stream of grain swiftly and frequently, to obtain a representative sample.

In Canada, the official inspection system covers grain, soyabeans, rapeseed and other products. Commodities are sold for export from the United States and Canada "by grade", determined at the time and place of loading into the ocean vessel. The required inspection certificate is final as between the parties. Soyabean meal is usually sold with sampling and analysis to be performed by an independent superintending firm (sometimes called "surveyor"), and its certificates are also accepted as final by buyer and seller. The parties may agree on other conditions, but the long-standing preference of the trade for sales with quality and condition final at loading stems from the reliance which buyers are willing to place on the accuracy of the certificate. Also if the goods must be disposed of on the market because they have arrived in poor condition, this can, *prima facie*, be accomplished more effectively by the buyer located in that market.

One exception to the finality of the certificate is in GAFTA 27 and 30, which provide that grain shipped in tankers or in the oil compartments of "ore/oil vessels" shall be subject to an allowance if it arrives at destination "damaged by seawater or otherwise". Commodities shipped in this manner are susceptible to loss of quality by reason of lack of proper aeration during the ocean voyage.

2. Commodities may be sold by sample which the seller has provided to the buyer. A sample is taken either at loading of the ocean vessel, or at discharge, depending on the terms of the contract, and it is compared with the contractual sample. Discrepancies in quality may call for the seller to pay discounts. If a settlement cannot be agreed amicably, the matter may be referred to arbitration. Rules for sampling are set forth in great detail in GAFTA contracts, as are the

rights of the parties to have new analyses performed if they are dissatisfied with the prior results.

3. Fair Average Quality ("FAQ") standards are arrived at by the trade association which analyses numerous samples received during the crop year. GAFTA describes the procedure as follows: "The Association has several committees which meet monthly and determine from the samples put before them the Fair Average Quality covering the many grains which are shipped."[2] To ascertain whether the shipment has met the FAQ requirements, a sample is taken of the physical goods and compared with the FAQ standards, which are regularly made public by the Association.

As we have indicated, U.S. and Canadian grains and related products are primarily sold with quality and condition final at loading. The buyer has the risk of deterioration of the goods during the ocean trip, from inherent vice, contamination by seawater, etc. The finality of the certificate is absolute, in the absence, naturally, of fraud or collusion. The English Court of Appeal considered the case of an official agency which realised, after being asked to review an inspection certificate, that a mistake had been made in the grading. It so advised the seller and final buyer. The documents had long since been negotiated and the court upheld the original certificate, even though issued in error, quoting from an earlier decision:

> "Whenever two persons agree together to refer a matter to a third person for decision, and further agree that his decision is to be final and binding upon them, then, so long as he arrives at his decision honestly and in good faith, the two parties are bound by it. They cannot reopen it for mistake or error on his part or for any reason other than for fraud or collusion."[3]

If the goods have been damaged through the fault of the vessel, the bill of lading holder may proceed against the vessel owner, or there may be recourse against the insurance underwriter. But marine insurance policies ordinarily do not provide coverage against the risks of inherent vice.

DELIVERY AND SHIPMENT PERIODS

The loading of grain into the ocean vessel is called a "delivery" in f.o.b. vessel contracts, and a "shipment" in c. and f./c.i.f. contracts.

[2] Pamphlet, *The World of GAFTA*—undated.

[3] *Alfred C. Toepfer* v. *Continental Grain Company* [1974] 1 Lloyd's Rep. 11 *et seq*.

There are clauses providing for the extension of the delivery or shipment periods in the NAEGA 2, GAFTA 64, 27 and 30, and FOSFA 24 contracts, which govern the exportation of grain and soyabeans from the United States and Canada. But if the commodity is not loaded to the ocean vessel by the original (or the extended) deadline, the party responsible may be called in default unless it has a valid excuse.

Expressions such as "quick" or "prompt" shipment are used in domestic, but not in international trading of grain, oilseeds and similar commodities. The contracts do, however, define "first half" and "last half" of a month of shipment as meaning, in the case of a month with an odd number of days, that the middle day of the month belongs to each half, i.e., first half December and last half December signify, respectively, December 1 to 16 and December 16 to 31.

The f.o.b. vessel seller under NAEGA 2 is not obliged to make delivery to the vessel until the latest of the following:

1. The first day of the established delivery period.
2. The expiration of the pre-advice period.
3. The time at which the vessel enters the loading berth, according to its "turn" in the vessel line-up.

Under GAFTA 27 and 30, shipment is to be made "per bill(s) of lading dated or to be dated . . .". The seller is permitted to commence loading the vessel before the start of the shipment period, provided that the loading is continuous and the bill of lading must be dated within the shipment period. The bill of lading must be dated when the goods are on board.

Time of delivery or of shipment in contracts for the sale of these goods is regarded as "of the essence"—a sensible rule, since commodity prices fluctuate constantly. *Force majeure* can, of course, justify delays, but the rule is otherwise stringent. A judgment by the English Court of Appeal states: "In the light of what was said by their Lordships [in a House of Lords case] I think it can fairly be said that in mercantile contracts stipulations as to time not only may be, but usually are, to be treated as being 'of the essence of the contract', even though this is not expressly stated in the words of the contracts."[4]

F.o.b. vessel contracts are often made with a delivery period of a full month, to be "narrowed" to a 20-day span. The declaration must

[4] *Bunge Corporation* v. *Tradax Export S.A.* [1980] 1 Lloyd's Rep. 294.

be made by the first day of the month preceding the month of delivery. The "narrowed period" is also called the "established" delivery period; it then governs the time in which the goods are to be loaded.

The NAEGA 2 contract provides that if a buyer's vessel has not tendered valid notice of readiness and has not filed a berth application by the end of the delivery period, the buyer is in breach of contract, and is liable for the payment of carrying charges to the seller.

NAEGA 2 affords the buyer automatic extensions, before it can be called in default:

1. A vessel nomination may be given as late as the fifteenth day after the last day of the established delivery period.
2. A nominated vessel may tender notice of readiness to load as late as the thirty-fifth day after the last day of the established delivery period.

There is special provision for deliveries at the Great Lakes, St. Lawrence, or Hudson Bay ports.

If the buyer is in breach for failure to meet these deadlines, the seller has the option of continuing to carry the grain with entitlement to carrying charges, or of tendering warehouse receipts to the buyer, or of calling the buyer in default of contract.

GAFTA 64, the f.o.b. vessel contract, allows the buyer an additional 21 days for delivery, provided a notice is sent to the seller not later than the business day following the last day of the original delivery period. During this extension period, the buyer must pay the seller carrying charges. This contract, unlike NAEGA 2, allows the seller to suspend delivery on the last day of the delivery period (or of the extended period).

Extensions for f.o.b. vessel contracts are generally more liberal than those for c. and f./c.i.f. contracts. F.o.b. vessel terms involve, essentially, the performance of the buyer in making available a ship for loading, and of the seller in delivering the commodity. C. and f./c.i.f. deliveries require mainly the performance of the seller, which must accomplish both of these functions, and which presumably has more control over the necessary logistics. GAFTA 27 and 30 allow the seller an additional eight days in which to effect shipment, provided that notice is given to the buyer not later than the business day following the last day of the shipment period. If an extension is claimed, the seller may still ship by the original deadline, but if it does not, it must pay an allowance to the buyer, on a sliding scale, which runs up to $1\frac{1}{2}\%$ of the c.i.f. value of the goods, for a delay of seven or eight days. If the vessel is not loaded within the eight days, the seller may be held in default. FOSFA 24's clause is similar to GAFTA's, but it is applicable only to contracts with shipment periods of no more than 31 days. Extensions of shipment appear in contracts issued by official buyers, occasionally with the same text as GAFTA's.

Grain is sometimes sold for arrival at the discharge port within a stipulated period, rather than for delivery at the port of loading within a particular span of time. The Common Agricultural Policy of the European Economic Community is the *raison d'être* for some of these sales, as it makes the importers pay levies, which insulate the relatively high prices within the Common Market, from the lower, world-market levels. These impositions are contracted for on the basis of stipulated arrival periods of the vessel in EEC ports. If a valid excuse cannot be given for the delayed arrival of a ship, the importer is subject to a penalty. A grain contract calling for arrival dates should envisage the possibility of a casualty to the vessel, which would presumably be considered an event of *force majeure* by the Common Market; there should be provision for payment in the event that the cargo is lost at sea.

There are no restrictions in NAEGA 2 concerning the type of vessel to be nominated by the buyer, although the parties usually have a specific agreement on this point, as there is a great difference in the speed (cadence) with which a bulk carrier, equipped for fast operations, can be loaded and discharged, as against a tanker or a "tweendecker". Addendum 1 to NAEGA 2 does specify that the loading rate guarantee applies only if the buyer nominates a self-trimming bulk carrier to lift the entire quantity of the contract, i.e., the guarantee is not effective for other types of ships, or if more than one bulker is nominated. This provision may, of course, be voided by the parties, or be amended by them, as is true of all of the terms of standard contracts.

The c. and f./c.i.f. contracts stipulate that shipment must be made by vessels with top classification in official ships' registers. As in f.o.b. vessel contracts, buyer and seller usually specify the type of ship which is to fulfil the contract, since the discharge ports are sometimes restricted as to draught, which may necessitate that the vessel be "lightened" before entering the loading berth, etc. Speed of discharge is an important consideration. Under the GAFTA contracts, the voyage is to be made "direct or indirect, with or without transhipment". If the goods are to be transhipped, this must be done under a "through" bill of lading.

A vessel's empty holds or a shipment of grain may have to be treated because of the presence of weevils. Some destinations invariably require that a solution of Malathion be sprayed over the grain while it is on a moving belt, before loading into the vessel. Malathion kills insects on contact. Fumigation may be carried out by releasing a gas in the vessel's holds, the ship having to remain in port until it is determined that the gas has dissipated and no longer constitutes a danger to the crew or shore personnel. Fumigation may be accomplished during the ship's voyage, without the necessity of holding it at anchorage, with the use of "blankets" of aluminium phosphide, which are placed in the holds after loading; their contents form a gas which permeates the grain. The necessary precautions are taken at the port of discharge to avoid any risk to personnel. Before fumigation takes place the vessel's holds will have been examined to make certain that they are airtight, and there is no danger that gas will leak out to other parts of the ship.

PRE-ADVICE OF VESSEL NOMINATIONS–F.O.B. VESSEL CONTRACTS

In f.o.b. vessel contracts, the buyer must give advance notice of the vessel nomination. This pre-advice is set by agreement, usually at 10 days for shipments of grain from the United States; under NAEGA 2, while the pre-advice is running, the seller has no obligation to have the vessel called into berth and to effect delivery. The pre-advice may be regarded as allowing the seller time for placing the commodity in loading position.

NAEGA 2 stipulates that the pre-advice starts running on the day when the seller has received the nomination. If the time of receipt is after 4 p.m., the notice is deemed received on the next business day. If the buyer and seller are both located in the Continental United States and/or Canada, this deadline for receipt is 4 p.m. *New York time*. A seller may receive a nomination just prior to 4 p.m., and be unable to pass it along to its own seller so that the latter receives it before the deadline. The party in such a fix, although innocent of any negligence, may be held responsible for costs or damages. If the nomination was received on a Friday and effectively passed along on Monday, the loss of the three days could result in a similar delay in the designation of the loading port or berth. If the vessel's filing with the loading elevator is deferred, the party having held up the vessel nomination is liable for the resulting demurrage or loss of despatch.

Under NAEGA 2, the custom of the port and the elevator tariff determine the sequence in which vessels will be loaded. In the past, some tariffs have given priority to liners, as against tramp vessels. Tramps themselves loading grain in the United States have, under normal circumstances, an order of preference (sometimes called order of rotation) corresponding to the date of their filing with the elevator. The charter-party (or contract of affreightment between the owner of the vessel and the charterer) requires that the vessel (or its agent) give the charterer (or its agent) the notice of readiness to load, along with the certificates of the National Cargo Bureau and the Federal Grain Inspection Service. This advice is, however, not directed to the elevator, with which the vessel is required to file a berth application so as to be placed in the "line-up". The "line-up" is simply the list of vessels waiting for an open berth, shown in the order in which they filed with the elevator. When a number of vessels are waiting for a berth, there is said to be "congestion at the berth". The ships are not physically in line or clogging the berth as the expressions "line-up" and "congestion" may imply. They may be tied up at lay or waiting berths or at anchorage, rather than at or off the elevator's docks.

Under NAEGA 2, if a vessel has become incapacitated, the buyer may substitute another. There is also a limited right to substitute one vessel if no casualty has taken place.

CARRYING CHARGES–F.O.B. VESSEL CONTRACTS

Under NAEGA 2, carrying charges are construed as being in the nature of liquidated damages payable by the buyer which has breached the contract. This breach results from the failure of the buyer's vessel to tender notice of readiness and to file with the loading elevator before the end of the established delivery period. The carrying charges consist of storage and of interest, at rates which are agreed upon by the buyer and seller. As the commodity is delivered to the vessel, the seller's cost of carrying the goods in storage terminates. Accordingly, storage is computed from the day following the established delivery period, up to the respective days of physical deliveries to the ship. If the established delivery period is December 1–21, and 15,000 tons are loaded on December 23, and 10,000 tons on December 24, storage charges will run from December 22 to 23 (both dates inclusive) for 15,000 tons and to December 24 for 10,000 tons. Interest charges, on the other hand, accrue for the entire delivery, up to the last day of loading under the contract. The logic of this provision is that it is normal for documents to be established and presented on completion of loading, and the seller is thus entitled to interest charges up to that time.

NOTICE OF APPROPRIATION AND NOTICE OF DELIVERY

The seller in a c. and f./c.i.f. contract must give the buyer a notice of appropriation (called Declaration of Shipment in FOSFA contracts), providing vessel name, quantity loaded, bill of lading date(s), commodity description and contract identification. This advice is important in several ways. It is the first notice to the buyer of the carrying vessel, the time of loading, and the quantity loaded. It allows the buyer to arrange for payment and for receipt of the goods, also possibly for their resale. If the buyer is a consumer (flour mill, compounder or crusher), this information may be important to the running of the industrial operation. The notice of appropriation or "tender" tells the buyer that a contract has been wholly or partly fulfilled; and that the seller need only present documents in proper order against payment, to complete its obligations for that shipment. The appropriation is open to correction of certain errors, but it is technically "unconditional" and may not be withdrawn. Its cancellation might result in confusion and possibly hardship to the buyer. Under English law, an unconditional appropriation transfers title from the seller to the buyer. Failure to appropriate the goods *per se* is grounds for a buyer's refusal to lift the documents and may result in the seller being declared in default of contract, even if the goods have been duly shipped and proper documents have been presented for payment. The rule makes commercial sense: it prevents the seller from waiting to declare the shipment until documents are tendered, and for using the interval for manoeuvres, such as resale of the goods "afloat" on the market, and application of a later shipment to the contract, against the buyer's interest. The appropriation must be made within a stipulated number of days after the bill of lading date, and must be passed on as prescribed.

The matter does not end with the seller's responsibility to tender the notice of appropriation timeously. A landmark case decided in 1977,[5] concerned a shipment with bill of lading dated April 4, 1973, which was appropriated by a party which we will call X, on May 16, 1973, well after the deadline. The notice was passed along that same day by X to Y, which received it on May 17, 1973, and rejected it with the words, ". . . Is this understood as a joke? Remind you 1st April has passed since long . . .". X maintained that the bill of lading was dated within the delivery period, and that under the contract Y was entitled to ask for "proof of string" (i.e., the listing of the parties in string commencing with the supplier of the physical grain), but that Y was not entitled to reject the appropriation. The ruling contract was GAFTA 100, which called for the first appropriation (i.e., by the supplier), to be made within 10 days of the bill of lading, and subsequent parties in string were to pass along the notice on the date of receipt, or on the next business day if received after 4 p.m. The court decided that: "It is for the sellers to prove on the balance of probabilities that every seller despatched his notice of appropriation in time and that the notice is therefore good." The advice, even though passed along without delay by X, was declared invalid. This outcome may seem a little harsh at first sight, but it does no more than preserve the obligations of the contract, and protect the ultimate buyer from receiving an appropriation which has been unduly delayed. Parties in string routinely receiving an appropriation ask the seller to provide a list of the previous parties and the date they gave the notice of appropriation.

As we have seen, GAFTA and FOSFA contracts require the appropriation to be passed along on the same day, if received prior to 4 p.m., otherwise on the next business day. FOSFA merely requires the passing along "with due despatch".

The seller under NAEGA contracts must give the buyer a notice of delivery which is similar in content to a notice of appropriation. Its legal effect, however, is different, as risk of loss passes to the buyer

[5] *Tradax Export S.A.* v. *Andre & Cie. S.A.* [1977] 2 Lloyd's Rep. 484.

upon the grain reaching the end of the elevator's loading spout, on its way to the vessel's hold, and title passes upon payment for the goods. Since the vessel is chartered (or possibly owned), by the buyer, the latter would presumably be informed of the loading in any event. Nonetheless, the notice is important, and particularly so to the members of a string having to settle up with their contract partners.

SHIPPING DOCUMENTS

An English authority[6] says, after considering alternative formulations, that it is probably correct to talk about a contract as being "for the sale of goods to be performed by the delivery of documents". Be that as it may, payment is made, not for the goods themselves, but against presentation of shipping documents. GAFTA 30 recites, "[p]ayment to be in cash in . . . [locale of payment] in exchange for Shipping Documents . . .". Variants may be used, such as "payment: by net cash in payment of and in exchange for shipping documents". This concept is so taken for granted, that its significance may be overlooked.

Shipping documents entitle their holder to obtain delivery of the goods from the vessel. They substantiate compliance with the contract terms as to time of delivery, place of delivery, quantity and quality specifications, etc. The buyer or its designee (e.g., a bank) examines the documents before effecting payment to ascertain that the seller has fulfilled its obligations under the contract. If the documents are in order, the seller has discharged its responsibility, except perhaps for adjustments such as accounting for shortages at discharge under a full outturn guarantee. Final invoices are also supported by certificates.

We have said that payment against documents is not payment against the goods themselves. If the vessel has sunk, payment may nonetheless still be due. Collection for documents may be made in various ways: under a letter of credit where the bank pays by honouring the drawing (draft and documents); through a bank (but not under a letter of credit); by payment on presentation directly to the buyer; or there may be an *acceptance* of a draft drawn to mature at a future date, etc.

[6] David M. Sassoon, *CIF and FOB Contracts*, 2nd ed., *British Shipping Laws*, Vol. 5 (London: Stevens & Sons, 1975), p. 23.

The documents include an invoice rendered by the seller and a mate's receipt or bills of lading. The mate's receipt is the document entitling its holder to claim delivery of the bills of lading from the vessel owner; it is a receipt for the goods loaded on board the vessel. If the charter-party requires the freight moneys to be prepaid, the ladings are released by the owner against such payment *and* surrender of the mate's receipt. NAEGA 2 gives the seller the option to submit either mate's receipt or bills of lading to the buyer for payment.

Mate's receipts are not issued for vessels loading at Canadian St. Lawrence ports. In the United States, the mate's receipt is accompanied by weight and inspection certificates when surrendered to the buyer or its agent at the port of loading, against payment. The buyer may not have an agent at the port of loading to take possession of the mate's receipt and surrender it to the owner against the bill of lading. Accordingly, NAEGA 2 states that "if practicable, seller shall follow the instructions of buyer in establishing bills of lading containing such clauses as buyer's/vessel's agents usually endorse or attach. Buyer shall accept such bills of lading but seller assumes no responsibility for their correctness." Delays may occur if the charter-party calls for the freight to be "prepaid". If the freight is not paid to the owner, the seller cannot obtain the ladings which are needed to effect collection; some contracts provide that the buyer is liable for interest if this occurs. We have said that the seller is entitled, under NAEGA 2, to submit the mate's receipt if the ladings cannot be obtained. This option is, however, theoretical when payment is by letter of credit which does not permit mate's receipts to be submitted in lieu of bills of lading.

Bills of lading ordinarily carry an "on-board" clause which is dated on the last day of loading. The ladings may further state that the weight of the goods in bulk was declared by the shipper, but certain "clauses" may impair the negotiability of the document and may be grounds for rejection by the buyer. The Uniform Customs and Practice for Documentary Credits, which constitute the ground rules followed by banks in interpreting letters of credit, read in Article 18, "[a] clean shipping document is one which bears no superimposed clause or notation which expressly declares a defective condition of the goods and/or the packaging";[7] banks will refuse documents

[7] In the Uniform Customs, which become effective in October 1984 (International Chamber of Commerce Publication No. 400), this clause is numbered 34, and "shipping document" appears as "transport document".

bearing such notations. Thus, the bills of lading must be "clean on-board".

Ladings are ordinarily issued in three originals; when one of these is surrendered to the vessel owner, the other two become invalid. The practice harks back to the uncertainty of the mails when ocean travel was hazardous. By issuing three originals, it could reasonably be expected that at least one would safely reach the buyer. The ladings may be issued "to order", which makes them transferable by endorsement. In some active reseller's markets, the ladings are subdivided into delivery orders, which are surrendered to the vessel owner.

In the grain trade shipments are generally made in tramp vessels, for which the contract of affreightment is called a charter-party. When the documents are negotiated, the holder of the bills of lading steps into the shoes of the charterer *vis-à-vis* the vessel owner. If the master causes the vessel to deviate in a manner not permitted under the charter-party, or violates the contract of affreightment in another way, the holder of the lading may take legal action.

The documentation required of the seller depends on the commodity, the destination and the type of sale (f.o.b., c. and f., c.i.f.). Documents such as weight and inspection certificates are issued by independent and reliable third parties, agreed to by the buyer and seller. U.S. grain covered by official grain standards must be inspected by, or under the supervision of, FGIS, and all grain shipped from Canada is subject to the inspection of the Canadian Grain Commission. If a sale of U.S. grain is made without any reference to official grade designations or factors, a waiver may be obtained from official (FGIS) inspection. Other documents may be phytosanitary certificate, protein certificate, certificate of origin, etc., as specified in the particular or standard contract language, in tender terms and in letters of credit.

PAYMENT TERMS

The world trade in grain is still essentially a cash affair, and extension of financing by the seller is rare, although on the increase. Generally, when financing is extended, the risk is transferred by the seller to a financial institution or a government agency. The U.S. Government has several programmes to encourage exports. Title I of Public Law 480 grants generous conditions to underdeveloped countries, with maturities of the order of 20 years, grace periods of 10 years, and low interest rates. The U.S. Department of Agriculture supplies export credit insurance under GSM–102, as well as a programme of "blended credit", for maturities of up to three years. The exporter receives payment after delivery, and does not assume the burden of financing.

Payment terms for a given transaction vary according to the country of destination and, in a lesser degree, the buyer. Sales to Western Europe are made for payment in cash against documents, sales to South American countries by irrevocable sight letter of credit, confirmed by a bank in the United States. Transactions between exporters in the United States are made for payment against mate's receipt.

The seller's best assurance of payment is in a sight documentary letter of credit opened irrevocably by a reliable bank in the United States, Canada or Western Europe—or confirmed by such a bank. Ideally, the letter of credit should be available almost immediately upon the sale being concluded. The deadline for the establishment of the letter of credit (called simply "credit") is almost always later than this, but it should be prior to the beginning of the delivery period. Having in hand a credit for which a reliable bank undertakes to honour drawings, ensures that delivery may be made with the certainty that payment will be forthcoming. If the contract calls for payment by letter of credit, the seller is under no obligation to deliver the goods unless and until a credit in proper order has been received. The contractual requirement of a letter of credit does not eliminate all risk to the seller, as the credit may never be opened, and the seller may accordingly have to forgo making shipment. A market loss may be incurred, amounting to the difference between the contract price and a lower market value. This risk is eliminated if the credit is opened simultaneously with making the sale, but this, as we have said, is not practicable.

A contractual requirement that the buyer open a letter of credit is not sufficient to ensure payment. This fact is demonstrated by the default of the Turkish purchasing agency, which caused a severe loss to the seller.

The terminology of credits may be briefly explained with an illustration. Company X in Latin America has purchased grain from

Company Y in the United States. X applies to its local bank for the opening of an irrevocable sight documentary credit in favour of Y, to be confirmed by a bank in the United States. With respect to the credit, X is called the account party, Y the beneficiary, X's local bank, the opening bank, the bank in the United States, the confirming bank. If the credit were advised instead of being confirmed, the bank in the United States would be styled the advising bank. If the confirming or advising bank pays the beneficiary, it is also called the paying bank. The terms of the letter of credit may be changed by amendment, and the credit is said to be negotiated or drawn against when drafts are presented by the beneficiary to the paying bank.

Credits may be revocable or irrevocable. Revocable credits may be amended or cancelled prior to negotiation, without the beneficiary's consent. In issuing an irrevocable credit, a bank commits itself unconditionally to honour properly drawn drafts. The credit may not be withdrawn or amended without the beneficiary's consent.

Credits may be advised or confirmed. These expressions refer to actions of a bank other than the opening bank. The confirming or advising bank is, in most cases, also the paying bank. The advising bank does not engage (or commit itself) to honour drafts drawn against the credit it has advised, but once it has made payment, it cannot under ordinary circumstances claim return of the funds from the beneficiary. A confirming bank engages its liability to honour properly drawn drafts, regardless of the performance or non-performance of the opening bank. In our example, if Y is the beneficiary of an irrevocable credit confirmed by Bank A in the United States, Y looks exclusively to Bank A for payment of its drafts, and not to the opening bank.

Contracts may call for sight documentary credits, requiring the beneficiary to submit drafts drawn at sight and accompanied by specified shipping documents. In determining if the documents submitted by the beneficiary of the credit are acceptable, the bank will be guided only by whether they conform to the specifications of the credit itself and the terms of the International Chamber of Commerce's Uniform Customs and Practice for Documentary Credits. The bank is not charged with knowledge of the contract of sale, and is not responsible for contradictions between its terms and those of the letter of credit. Let us take the example of a contract for delivery March 1–16, whereas by an error, the credit stipulates March 10–16. The bank, having no cognisance of the agreement between buyer and seller, will be governed only by the delivery period in the credit. It is because banks rigorously follow the specifications of the credit in determining conformity of the documents that the credit must be carefully examined by the beneficiary upon receipt. Any errors or omissions should be swiftly brought to the attention of the buyer, with a request to have them corrected by amendment. A letter of credit with a discrepancy may render it not negotiable, and therefore of no practical value to the beneficiary until it is properly amended.

The Uniform Customs give definitions of terms, guidelines and rules for interpreting credits. They contain a section entitled "TRANSFER", which defines the procedure for making credits available to third parties for payment or acceptance. The rules state that, unless otherwise specified, charter-party bills of lading will be rejected by the bank; the charter-party might contain terms harmful to the account party (or buyer). The Uniform Customs define what the trade calls "stale documents", i.e., those submitted more than 21 days after the issue of the bills of lading, when there is no specific deadline on the credit. "Stale documents" are refused by the bank as they may occasion the account party (or buyer) expenses if the vessel is already in the port of discharge by the time the documents are sighted. These illustrations give only a bare idea of the Uniform Customs, which are quite comprehensive.

We have discussed sight documentary letters of credit, and must now study acceptance credits, also called usance credits, utilised when buyers desire commercial bank financing. To the seller, this type of financing may be tantamount to a sight credit if the drafts are discountable. The acceptance or usance credit calls for the presentation of drafts (accompanied by specified shipping documents), maturing, not at sight, but at a stated number of days or months after sight. If the drawing has been made with the proper documentation, the bank will mark it "ACCEPTED", will sign it and will return it to the beneficiary. This draft is called an acceptance and may be discounted ("sold" for cash), either by the accepting bank or by another financial institution; or it may be held by the beneficiary for presentation and payment at maturity. In some countries, the acceptance of a draft by a bank is called an "*aval*". If the credit was opened irrevocably or confirmed by a prime accepting bank, and if the bank accepted it without recourse, the beneficiary's risk is effectively eliminated upon discounting.

The allocation of bank charges incurred with respect to credits, as between buyer and seller, should be spelled out in the contract. It is generally understood that if payment is to be by irrevocable confirmed sight documentary credit, the bank charges will be for account of the buyer. It is nonetheless advisable for the contract of sale to be specific on this point. Precision in the contract is even more necessary with usance credits, where there are several types of charges. The opening fee is charged by the opening bank for establishing the credit. The confirmation or advising fee is obviously assessed by the confirming or advising bank. The accepting bank imposes a fee for lending its name or accepting the drafts; the discount charge is the cost of discounting or buying the accepted drafts. Buyer and seller may agree, for example, that the drafts are to include a specified interest rate, that the acceptance fee will be borne by the buyer and the discount charges, by the seller. Whatever terms may be agreed between the parties, the resulting bank charges payable by the seller will presumably have been calculated in the offering price.

Payment "CAD" or cash against documents signifies that the buyer is to pay upon presentation of documents. The time and place of presentation must be stated in the contract, there must be an understanding as to what shipping documents must be submitted, and the method of payment should be set forth. If the time is not specified, presentation may be made at seller's option after delivery of the goods, but undue delay may make the seller liable for expenses incurred by the buyer. For instance, the vessel may have arrived at the port of discharge in the interim, necessitating that the buyer or receiver post a bond in order to obtain delivery of the goods; if the goods must be warehoused awaiting receipt of the documents, storage expenses will accrue. The contract may call for payment to be made on vessel's arrival at the port of discharge, but in any event not later (or earlier) than a given deadline (see page 12). The best formulation of this proviso is that payment is to be made against presentation, on vessel's arrival at the discharge port, of a sight draft accompanied by documents; but the presentation may be made on or after a stated number of days following the bill of lading date if the ship has not arrived by then.

The place of presentation may be the buyer's domicile for c. and f./c.i.f. sales, and the seller's, for f.o.b. vessel sales, but this is entirely a matter of agreement between the parties. The documents are spelled out in the contract, or they may be regulated by custom of the trade. They may be presented directly to the buyer, or, more generally, through the seller's bank, which presents them to the buyer through a correspondent bank in the buyer's country. When interest rates are high, there is an incentive for the seller to present the drawing as soon as possible, perhaps by having them sent by courier overseas for presentation through a bank with the same domicile as the buyer, or through a local commercial agent of the seller.

Collection charges assessed by a bank in the seller's country are generally for seller's account, and banking fees in the buyer's country, for buyer's account. The buyer must pay any fees required for obtaining the foreign exchange necessary to make the payment. The actual remittance may be by telegraphic transfer to a bank designated by the seller, in federal funds, by certified cheque, etc. Variations in payment methods depend largely on the country of purchase and the purchaser. Some foreign buyers have an arrangement with banks in New York, which advise the buyer by telex when the documents have been received in proper order from the seller. The buyer then instructs the bank to effect payment; meantime the drawing is held by the bank in New York. These different means of payment afford protection to the seller in that the documents are not released to the buyer until remittance is made, but, as we have pointed out in the case of letters of credit, they do not eliminate the market risk created when the drawing is not honoured, i.e., the loss resulting from the market value being lower than the contract price at the time the goods must be disposed of to a third party. The defaulter must make good this loss to its seller, but actual recovery may be an arduous task. Government programmes do not automatically eliminate the seller's exposure. Title I of Public Law 480, for instance, cautions that any delivery made prior to receipt of the letter of credit, remains at the seller's risk. If a buyer of grain financed under GSM-102 fails to nominate a vessel, the seller's recourse is not against the government, but against the buyer, in the same manner as if no government guarantee were involved.

"BASIS" TRADING

"Basis" trading is a long-standing, routine procedure for the American grain community. It is a natural outgrowth of hedging, which in turn was made possible by the development in the United States of efficient futures markets. Basis trading is spreading throughout the world, and even official purchasing entities have taken to utilising this pricing mechanism.

"Basis" trading is likely to seem a mysterious phenomenon to those who do not understand hedging. The latter is a technique which aims to reduce the market risk in the trading of commodities; the risk is largely a function of the time element. Were physical grain always purchased and sold simultaneously, there would be no need to hedge as there would be no exposure to loss caused by market rises or declines. Processors and merchandising firms which store, condition and ship grain must hedge, or eventually face very large losses which could bankrupt them. If grain is purchased and carried in inventory for a few weeks, its value is likely to be quite different from the original purchase price. Hedging is basically a process designed to overcome or minimise the gap in time between purchases and sales of physical (or "cash") grain. It consists simply of the purchase of futures contracts when selling cash grain, and vice-versa. It is not always possible (nor is it always desirable) to purchase and sell cash grain at the same time; the next best protection is the substitution in the equation of futures for cash grain. Hedging, it must be observed, lessens the market risk, but does not eliminate it; it aims at restricting this exposure *to the basis*, rather than having it play upon the more volatile flat price.

Let us assume that the author of this book, and the reader, own a merchandising operation, and that we intend to purchase and sell cash grain, hedging the transactions. We start by purchasing No. 3 or better Yellow Corn, for delivery August 1–31, f.o.b. vessel Mississippi River ports. The prices per bushel which we pay for the cash grain, and those for the Chicago September futures which we sell, are:

Date	*Bushels*	*Flat prices paid for purchases of cash grain*	*Prices per bushel of futures sold*
June 15	500,000	\$3.50½	\$3.20¼
June 30	50,000	3.51¼	3.22⅛
July 11	100,000	3.50	3.19⅜
July 18	531,102*	3.51⅜	3.21
Total	1,181,102		
Weighted averages		\$3.50883	\$3.20592

* 530,000 bushels of futures were actually sold, not 531,102, as futures are regularly dealt with in 5,000 bushel lots, or multiples thereof.

The prices shown are per bushel; if you feel more comfortable with metric tons, use the conversion factor of 1 metric ton = 39.370079 bushels of corn. The "basis" or "premium" is the difference between the cash price and the futures, i.e., \$3.50883 per bushel, less \$3.20592, or \$0.30291 per bushel (equivalent to \$11.9256 per metric ton) over Chicago September futures.

Our position is now:

	bushels
Long Cash Grain—August 1–31 Delivery	1,181,102
Short Chicago September futures	1,180,000
Net Long	1,102

On July 20, we make *a sale of cash grain*, for 30,000 metric tons (1,181,102 bushels), 5% more or less, of No. 3 or better Yellow Corn, for delivery August 1–31, at \$3.52 per bushel, or \$138.58 per metric ton, f.o.b. vessel Mississippi River ports. Hedging requires a *contra* operation in the futures market whenever a purchase or sale is made. Purchasing futures will make our position even once again and, on July 20, we acquire:

500,000 bushels at	\$3.19$\frac{1}{2}$ per bushel
100,000 bushels at	3.19
200,000 bushels at	3.18$\frac{3}{4}$
300,000 bushels at	3.19$\frac{1}{8}$
80,000 bushels at	3.18$\frac{7}{8}$
Total 1,180,000	Weighted average \$3.21193

We have just bought 1,180,000 bushels of futures at a weighted average price of \$3.21193 per bushel. The basis for our sale is \$0.30807 per bushel. We may now calculate our profit:

	per bushel
FUTURES:	
Sold at	\$3.20592
Bought at	3.21193
Loss	\$0.00601
CASH GRAIN:	
Sold at	\$3.52
Bought at	3.50883
Gain	\$0.01117
NET GAIN	\$0.00516

The possible effect on our profit and loss of the unhedged amount of 1,102 bushels is not significant and we have ignored it.

It will be recalled that our position had been "long" cash grain, 1,181,102 bushels, and "short" 1,180,000 bushels of futures; our operations of July 20 have offset these amounts by *contra* transactions and we are "net even", viz., neither "long" nor "short". Our operations are now concluded.

Note that the net gain of $0.00516 per bushel may be arrived at more quickly by simply comparing the basis for our purchase with that for our sale of cash grain:

	per bushel
Actual basis for our sale	$0.30807
Actual basis for our purchase	0.30291
Gain	$0.00516

Traders hedging as a matter of course find it easier to do their reckoning with the basis rather than the flat price. The basis they use, however, is that which they calculated at the time of the purchase or sale, and not that computed on the actual futures covered, as in our examples.

While we have been purchasing futures, our buyer has been occupied in doing just the opposite, i.e., selling them. If the futures market had risen before we had been able to cover, we would have suffered a loss when buying them. Our buyer, on the other hand, would sustain a loss had the market declined.

We might have joined forces with our buyer, so as to avoid each of us entering the futures market separately. Instead of selling the corn at the flat price of $138.58 per metric ton, we might mutually have agreed on a basis (or premium) price, e.g., 30 cents over Chicago September futures. Our buyer would have agreed to surrender to us ("give up") 1,180,000 bushels (about 30,000 metric tons) of Chicago September corn futures, prior to expiration of trading of this futures month on the Exchange, and at the price ruling at the time of transfer. Let us say that the buyer "gave" us futures as follows:

1,180,000 bushels at $3.21½ per bushel.

The flat price is $3.51½ per bushel (or $138.386 per metric ton): $3.21½ + $0.30 per bushel, the contract basis. We will invoice the physical shipment of grain, when loaded into the vessel in August, at the price of $138.386 per metric ton.

(We have cheated a little, in order not to abuse your patience, by having the futures exchanged all at once for the entire quantity of 1,180,000 bushels; had this been done in several lots, at different prices, we would have had to compute the weighted average.)

Fluctuations in the values of futures "taken" from our buyer would not have affected our profit and loss. If the futures had been exchanged at \$3.25 per bushel, i.e., at $3\frac{1}{2}$ cents per bushel more than the price at which we did acquire them, we would have been compensated by a correspondingly higher invoice value for the cash grain which we sold (\$3.25 + \$0.30 = \$3.55 per bushel, or $3\frac{1}{2}$ cents less than the actual flat price of \$3.51$\frac{1}{2}$ per bushel).

In exchanges of futures, rather than having buyer and seller operate independently, both parties benefit from this procedure through a reduction in futures brokerage fees, and the ability to operate in that market without fearing price swings which could create losses. Also, the market exposure is limited to the basis (32 cents or \$12.598 per metric ton), instead of the more hazardous flat price of \$138.58 per metric ton.

The contract may call *for us*, the sellers, to buy the futures for our purchaser upon its instructions, instead of "taking" them from the buyer. The buyer is then speculating that the futures price will decline between the date of the transaction and the date of the instructions; the flat price will, of course, reflect any decrease in the futures. Or, again, the contract may simply call for our buyer to instruct us when to fix the futures (or "spot the board"), thus setting the cash price without our being obligated to accept or to purchase futures.

We have said that the aim of hedging is to reduce the trader's exposure to fluctuations *in the basis*, rather than in the flat price. In our joint venture, dear reader, the basis was around 30 cents per bushel over the futures price; the flat price was about \$3.50 per bushel. A fluctuation of 10 % in the basis would result in a small rise or fall of 3 cents per bushel; a similar percentage reckoned on the flat price yields 35 cents per bushel. In practice, too, the basis *tends* to be much more stable than the flat price. Nonetheless, the basis *is* capable of rapid and pronounced movement up or down. Hedging may also be bedeviled by the impossibility of entering into the futures market simultaneously with making a cash transaction. This happens when the cash transaction is made while the futures market is not in session, or when prices, at the opening of the futures market, rise or fall the full permissible limit, and no trading takes place for a while. When trading resumes, the prices may be quite different than when the cash trade was entered into. For all its weaknesses, though, hedging is a *sine qua non* for the industry, and without it, few active traders of cash grain would survive for long.

Paradoxically, basis trading may be the means for the purchaser to speculate. If futures are not acquired and given to the seller, the buyer takes a chance on the flat price alone, and is subject to the vagaries of the market. This might suit a buyer with a bearish outlook on the futures, and with a tolerance for substantial risks.

Since swings in the basis are generally more moderate than those in futures, a procurement agency may find it desirable to make basis purchases, if it must purchase ahead of being able to sell to processors or millers. It will thereby limit potential losses.

Some of the points which should be covered in contracts for basis trading are:

1. It should be made clear how the futures are to be fixed—by exchange, i.e., by the purchaser surrendering them to the seller. Or by the seller acquiring them on instructions of the buyer. Or by the seller "spotting the board".

2. The deadline for fixing the futures should be stated. This might be the expiry of the futures month on the Exchange, or the commencement of the delivery date for the physical grain, whichever last occurs. If the futures may be fixed *after* the delivery of the cash grain, provision for margin may be desirable; this is a deposit maintained by the buyer with the seller, to secure the latter whenever the futures market rises above the futures price used in the provisional invoice for the cash grain delivered to vessel.

3. If the seller is not to receive futures from the buyer, exact terms should be spelled out for the timing of the orders to buy the futures, e.g., prior to the opening of the Exchange, and if so, how long before? The seller's order may not be fulfilled even though the market briefly reached the required level, as earlier orders are executed first. There must be an understanding as to what the liability of the seller is, if the futures cannot be covered on behalf of the buyer, in accordance with the latter's instructions.

4. Provision should be made in case the buyer does not give up the futures, or fails to give orders for the seller to buy them or to "spot the board". The seller might be given the right to act for the buyer in this respect.

PRO RATA CLAUSE—C. AND F./C.I.F. CONTRACTS

When a vessel carries parcels of the same commodity specifications sold to different buyers, the physical separation of each lot on board can be achieved in two ways. "Natural" separation assigns the entire contents of each hold to one sales contract only. This is not very practical, as it is unlikely that the quantity in each hold will match up with individual sales. Also the elevator facilities and procedures at loading make it difficult to determine the weight of the commodity in any given hold. The alternative is to establish "artificial" separations within the holds, so as to keep the lots apart during the voyage and the unloading at destination. Japanese contracts JF–1 and JSB–2 call for natural separations of lots loaded on the vessel, but "in case of absolute necessity", allow one physical separation (Kobe type) per hold, of "a sturdy construction, flatly built with tarpaulin or roofing paper spread over an even base and then covered with thick dunnage boards, so that the machine discharge work on the upper cargo may be performed".

The identification of individual lots sold to different parties for discharge at the same port is not practicable by natural separations; artificial ones involve expenses for the material used, its installation, and the loss of time in loading and discharge. The goods may become commingled because of accidental damage to the separations in the course of discharging. The simple answer provided by the English contracts is that the lots need not be physically separated at all. FOSFA 24 reads: "Should any of the [contract] quantity form part of a larger quantity of the same or different period of shipment or of similar quality, no separation or distinction shall be necessary." Incidentally, GAFTA 30 has preserved a reference, now anachronistic, to shipment in bags.

Since the *pro rata* clauses, as they are called, eliminate the need for physical distinctions between the lots, how is one to apportion the commodity among the various buyers or receivers at discharge? *Pro rata* procedures have been established in detail for several Continental ports, dealing with such questions as—how are shortages between the weights at loading and discharge to be allocated among the receivers? How are "loose collected, damaged goods and sweepings" (GAFTA 30) to be distributed?

The *pro rata* clauses deal with a vexing problem in a practical and fair manner.

STRINGS AND CIRCLES

If we could accompany a shipment of grain from the place of production in the United States to the processing plant overseas, we might be starting out at a silo on a Midwestern farm and going by truck to a country elevator, thence to an installation on a river. A trip by barge would take us to an export elevator on the Mississippi, near the Gulf of Mexico. From there we would sail to an overseas port, where we would unceremoniously be dropped into a barge, to be conveyed to the feed manufacturing plant. During all this time, the grain would be bought and sold by several firms in the United States and overseas. This process would commence with the country station's acquisition of the grain from the farmer, and its sale to the operator of the river house. The physical grain would quickly become unidentifiable: it is mingled with grain of similar quality and it is dried, blended and shipped with the intention of meeting contract standards, its origin being of no consequence. Along the way, our lot will have been dumped into a bin with product of the same characteristics, and will have become indistinguishable from the neighboring kernels. Especially-prized varieties of grain or, more likely, oilseeds, are sometimes handled on an "identity-preserved" basis, and care is then taken to prevent their admixture with other commodities.

One might think of the various firms trading our lot as being "in string"; actually, however, this is not the case, at least from a formal standpoint.

Technically, a string is a series of transactions in which each of the parties, except the first and the last, is both a buyer and seller. The following is an example of a string of f.o.b. vessel contracts:

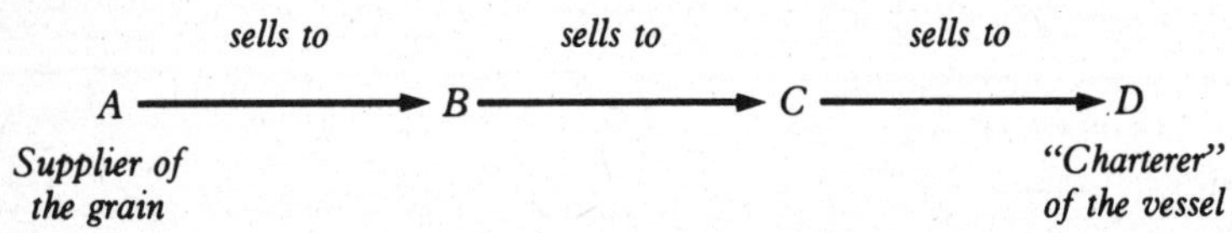

B and C are both buyers and sellers; A, exclusively a seller in the string, will be referred to as the supplier. D, exclusively a buyer, will be called the charterer—for the sake of convenience only, since D could be a reseller f.o.b. vessel under standard contract terms differing from those of the other transactions in the string, e.g., all sales might be under NAEGA 2 except for D's, which might be a f.o.b. vessel sale to the Soviet Union, and thus not subject to the terms of NAEGA 2. Each of the contracts involved in the string must be for a commodity of the same description, for delivery at the same port(s) (and/or shipment to the same port(s) in c. and f./c.i.f. sales), governed by the same standard terms, and with compatible quantities and delivery periods. The sale price will differ from contract to contract.

We now know that the lot of grain which became our traveling companion, was not bought and sold entirely "in string", although there may have been exceptions, e.g., there might have been a series of sales f.o.b. vessel qualifying as a string. Purchases and sales "of the same grain" are not trades "in string" unless the terms we have cited above (commodity, delivery point/s, etc.) are identical for the various transactions, or compatible.

In strings, one physical delivery of the commodity is applied to all the contracts. In the example above, D nominates a vessel with the quaint name of *Hopalong* to C, under a purchase from the latter. C does likewise with B, and B with A. The passing along of the nomination from D to A has produced a string. It is theoretically possible to create a string of f.o.b. vessel contracts *prior* to the nomination coming down the line, but this is not the practice. Firms are unwilling to "marry-off" particular purchases and sales earlier than necessary, as they do not wish to give up more favorable "matches" of contract which might arise later. After the vessel nomination reaches A, the latter will, if required by the contract, designate a loading port and/or berth; this information will be transmitted through the string to D, whose ship will, at the proper time, be ordered into berth for loading. When the vessel lifts the grain, a delivery notice is sent by A to B, and by B (as well as by each subsequent seller) to its buyer; thus, the one delivery notice is passed through the entire string, and the shipment of grain goes in satisfaction of all the contracts in string.

"Swinging markets" featuring great price swings are apt, of course, to generate a speculative fever, and in certain markets, this creates many "paper trades", transactions which tend to attract firms utilizing trades in physical grain instead of futures. Avoiding the futures markets also avoids having to deposit margins. When the activity in "paper" increases, so do strings, and so, parenthetically, do the problems created by the delays in transmission of notices through strings which have included upwards of 50 participants! The expression "paper" may give the wrong impression, in that it connotes theoretical rather than real trades. Non-speculators take part in this business as well as "swingers". Defaults, though rare, can usually be laid at the doorstep of the latter, which are often inordinate risk-takers.

Whether or not in string, the buyer or seller of grain is itself responsible for its own performance, and may not simply beg out of liability because someone else in the string has committed a breach. If vessel *Hopalong* omits to tender a notice of readiness and to file a berth application with the loading elevator, C will be in default vis-á-vis B, its seller, although C will have a separate cause of action against D; in fact, each seller in string will have recourse against its buyer. If there is sufficient time, a party may be able to make other arrangements for performance when it appears that it may be forced into a breach by the default of a string member. A new or existing contract may be substituted for the one which will not be executed; in most cases, however, one acquires the knowledge that a default will take place, only after the end of the delivery period, when it is too late to take action to substitute another contract. The principle that each contract stands on its own ("privity of contract", in lawyer's language) is a basic one, as one relies on the performance of the party one has chosen to do business with, and one should not be dependent on the actions of a firm one might not have wished to deal with, in the first place. The theory is that eventually, the party committing the breach is held liable. If A does not deliver the goods, A is in breach with respect to B, B to C, C to D. A ultimately bears the responsibility for the default. If A turns out to be bankrupt and unable to compensate B, this does not relieve B from having to pay C (and C from having to pay D). Since it was B which contracted with a party (A) which turned out to be insolvent, the consequences are visited on B, and not on the other string members.

There is a natural tendency to think that one's mere presence in a string eliminates risks of execution, since all claims received can be passed along. One unavoidable risk, however, is that of inability to transmit a notice effectively on the day of receipt. A vessel nomination received in the United States on a Friday at 2 p.m. New York time, is transmitted to the European seller 10 minutes later (e.g., at 7.10 p.m. European time). Under the terms of NAEGA 2, the deadline for receipt of this notice is 4 p.m. local time. Therefore, the nomination is deemed effective as of the following business day, Monday. Through no fault on its part, the unlucky firm having technically held up the notice, will suffer a loss if laytime under the loading rate guarantee commences earlier in its sale than in its purchase.

Defaults may also have untoward effects on string members which become innocent victims of someone else's breach, as the following example will show. Let us assume a string with three parties:

A ——————→ *B* ——————→ *C*

sale at $130/MT *sale at $140/MT*

The delivery period in each case is May 1–31. B waits vainly for a vessel nomination from C, which would be passed on to A. On June 16, A, the supplier, declares B in default. The market value is $145/MT, and A, having a gain as between the contract and the market prices, cannot claim damages from B. If B had thought that it had some immunity from problems of execution by reason of being in string, it is now disabused. B, having been held in default of contract by A, has no cause of action against the latter. B could hold C in default, but the damages would be nil, since the market price of $145/MT is greater than the adjusted sale price of $143/MT ($140/MT plus $3 in carrying charges from June 1 to the date of declaration of default). Even though B has acted with complete propriety, its paper gain of $10/MT has vanished, and with it, any illusion that being in string guarantees one from being caught "in the middle".

In strings of f.o.b. vessel contracts, the transmission of documents from party to party is inefficient and time-consuming. Arrangements are often made to by-pass some or all of the parties between the supplier and the charterer. The first seller in this agreement tenders the documents to the last buyer and obtains payment from the latter. The parties remit and collect amounts which give effect to the various contract prices. Carrying charges and demurrage/despatch under load rate guarantees are settled by each firm with its buyer and seller, and remain outside the arrangement. The *modus operandi* we have described is not referred to in NAEGA 2 and is altogether voluntary.

Strings of *c.i.f.* contracts appear from time to time; they are apt to cause even more serious problems than those for f.o.b. vessel transactions. C.i.f. strings are created only after the vessel has been loaded, and as the notices of appropriation are making their way toward the last buyer. There are bound to be delays transmitting the appropriation, especially between parties located on different continents. The goods arriving at the destination may have to be stored before the receivers can be identified. The documents trail the appropriation, and losses of interest are incurred by the firms which receive and pay for the documents but are unable to present them to their buyer on the same day.

The contracts make reference to strings only in connection with the passing along of certain notices, such as invocations of strike clauses. Circles, on the other hand, are dealt with at length. These are series of transactions in which each buyer, without exception, is also a seller of a commodity of the same description, for delivery at the same port(s) in f.o.b. vessel contracts, and shipment to the same port(s) in c. and f./c.i.f. contracts, governed by the same contract terms, with the same quantity and compatible delivery periods. Voluntary agreements may be made for the settling out of these contracts by payment of price differences, before physical delivery. The standard contracts provide a formula for payment if the parties do not arrive at a voluntary understanding. This is an elegant way of having the parties pay out the smallest amounts consistent with their obligations, and at the same time, of having them deal only with their actual buyer and seller, maintaining privity of contract. For those who enjoy arithmetical games, here is how the system works, under GAFTA 27 and 30. Each buyer must pay its seller the difference between the contract price and the lowest price in the circle. Let us say that A sells to B at $100 per metric ton, B to C at $105, C to D at $98, and D to A at $110. Applying the formula, B pays A $2 per metric ton, C pays B $7, D pays nothing, A pays D $12.

It will be seen that the net outlay of A is $10 per metric ton, (i.e., collecting $2 from B, and paying $12 to D), which corresponds to A's loss of $10, since it purchased at $110 and sold at $100. If B refuses to pay the $2, A may demand arbitration from B.

In bankruptcies, the calculation is different, inasmuch as GAFTA contracts require settlements at the market price. We must therefore apply a market value in settling out each contract, say $103 per metric ton, instead of the lowest invoice value. Our circle would require the following payments: A pays B $3 per metric ton, C pays B $2, D pays C $5, and A pays D $7. In this way, A again has paid out a net amount of $10, corresponding to its loss. If C is the bankrupt party, B will at

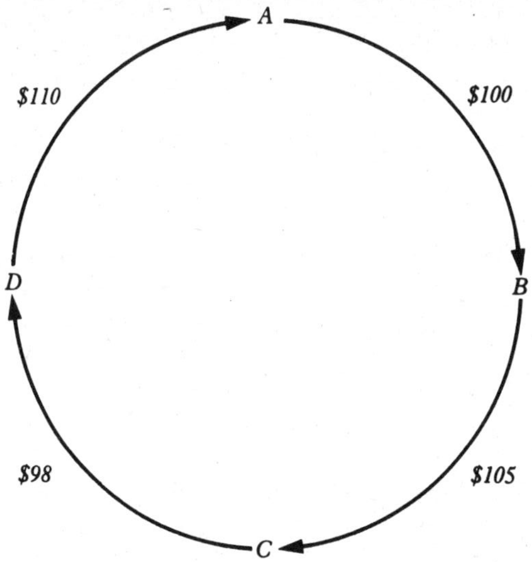

best recover only a portion of the $2 owed it by C. Since B chose to deal with C, B is properly required to shoulder the consequences of C's bankruptcy, rather than A, which had no contract with C, and which had never bargained for an exposure to C's bankruptcy.

Applying the bankruptcy rule to a circle may have important consequences. B might have started out in the circle as follows:

B owes A $2/ton, and C owes B $3/ton. Net owed to B, $1/ton. The bankruptcy of C having intervened, it became necessary to effect the settlements at the market price, and suddenly B finds itself in this situation:

B owes A $7/ton, and C owes B $8/ton. Net owed to B, $1/ton.

It will be noted that in each computation, C is to collect a net amount of $1/ton so that superficially, the net effect is unchanged. Unfortunately for B, however, the first calculation has B at risk with C for $3/ton, and this would have been the maximum extent of its loss, without the application of the special procedure for bankruptcies. In the new calculation, B is at risk for $8/ton, a far larger exposure. B must, of course, pay A the amount due it, regardless of C's insolvency.

The bankrupt party may not be disregarded in a circle settlement. Let us assume the following, in a bankruptcy settlement:

C, the bankrupt party, owes D \$5/ton, and is owed \$5/ton by B.

It would be nice to have B pay D \$5/ton, as if C had fortuitously vanished. Regrettably, this cannot be done. Instead, D will recover only a part, if any, of its \$5/ton, and B will have to pay \$5/ton into the "pot" to be shared by the creditors.

In ordinary circumstances, circles are settled by voluntary agreements, but the mechanism of the contracts is extremely useful in the few instances where it is needed. Great waste would result if each buyer had to pay the full value of its contract, rather than the difference between it and the lowest invoice value, or the market value.

NAEGA 2, taking its cue from its English cousins, has a similar circle clause. Various deadlines are stipulated in all the contracts as to remittances.

The parties to a circle may, if they wish, give notices of appropriation, and submit documents, or else arrange to forgo their presentation. The circle clauses specifically insure that parties will not be caught unawares and held in default by members which may be disingenuous or simply not informed that a circle exists.

BREACHES, DEFAULTS AND DAMAGES

In the normal course of business, the fact that the English contracts are subject to English law and NAEGA 2 to New York State law, seems theoretical. When difficulties occur, the best source of interpretation is, not surprisingly, the contract itself and the standard language which it incorporates. Trade organisations do not give interpretations of contract terms issued by them, much to the dismay of people seeking their guidance. The members of the contract committees are presumably most knowledgeable about the contracts. While they serve the associations without pay, they are employed by private firms, and have little leisure for consultations with members of the trade. But, much more importantly, the associations must not usurp the role of arbitrators, who act as the judiciary, so to speak, while the organisations issuing the standard language function in a legislative capacity. Opinions given in the name of the trade groups would be cited to arbitration panels as gospel, and would thus impinge on their authority. Furthermore, a technical question usually cannot be answered in a vacuum but must be analysed in the light of relevant facts; this is properly the domain of counsel.

Where terms are missing or ambiguous, it becomes necessary to turn to standards of interpretation or legal precepts. English commercial jurisprudence is embodied in rules of law established by precedent, i.e., by prior court cases. In New York State, the Uniform Commercial Code ("UCC") is the main, though not the sole, statutory guide. It contains a list of definitions and a series of rules of law, each accompanied by a commentary and illustrations. There has grown up around the Code a body of construction by courts and by leading jurists. Jurisprudence under English commercial law and under the UCC is evolving. For example, decisions under the Code have tended to give wider scope to consumer rights and to the doctrine of unconscionabilitv. The English, for their part, seem to make increasingly finer distinctions on certain legalistic points. Thus, a difference is now recognised between contractual conditions, warranties and innominmate terms. Non-performance of a condition entitles the injured party to hold the contract at an end. Breach of a warranty gives rise to claims for damages only. Failure to perform innominate (or intermediate) terms will have results which depend on the nature and consequences of the breach.

These references to the law may be daunting; yet most cases are solved correctly without requiring a profound study of the law. The reasonable, commercial answers are generally those which would be arrived at by systematic application of the legal tenets. Proved custom or usage of the trade may govern where the contract terms are unclear; this is not only an obvious practical approach, it is given full sanction under both systems. There are, of course, complex cases where only a careful review of the law will yield the answers.

Contractual duties may be ignored or violated in any number of ways, with varying results. For example, the seller may fail to effect delivery or to present a certain shipping document; the buyer may omit to nominate a vessel, or may delay payment. The standard contracts spell out obligations of the parties, but they do not generally list or describe breaches. NAEGA 2 does provide that a breach shall have occurred if the buyer does not, within the required deadlines, nominate a vessel or have the ship tender notice of readiness to load. GAFTA 27 and 30 state that if final invoices are not settled without delay, "a dispute shall be deemed to have arisen, which may be referred to arbitration".

An attempt to catalogue breaches and remedies in the contracts would be wearisome and fruitless. These are matters best settled by arbitration, where the relevant principles may be applied to the particular circumstances.

Failure to meet a contractual duty does not *per se* afford grounds for recovery of damages. The other party may have waived the right to claim a breach: if a notice of appropriation is received after the deadline, but the buyer offers no objection and accepts the documents without demur, an action cannot be brought against the seller for breach of contract.

A breach may be avoided if a seller "narrows" the delivery period of a f.o.b. vessel contract, after the buyer has failed to do so. The buyer may incur expenses as a result, e.g., for demurrage due the vessel owner if the "narrowed" period happens to commence after the vessel's arrival at the port of loading. NAEGA 2 is silent on the parties' rights, but it has been held that the seller may proceed in the manner described, and, having done so, it seems clear that it cannot claim a breach on the part of the buyer.

A breach may entitle the injured party to damages, without, however, excusing performance of the remaining duties. If, in a f.o.b. vessel sale, a ship is loaded out of proper rotation because of a non-contractual "bypass", the buyer may claim damages for a breach attributable to the seller, but the seller would not be excused from presenting the documents, or the buyer from paying for them.

Some breaches are of so severe a nature that they not only permit the injured party to ask for damages, but also excuse it from further performance. These are the "defaults" referred to by the English contracts and by NAEGA 2. A purchaser undertakes to open a documentary letter of credit in favour of the seller not later than 10 days before the commencement of the delivery period, but the credit is not opened at all. The duty breached is so fundamental that the seller may invoke the default clause, claiming damages, without having to effect delivery. Legally, the establishment of the letter of credit was a condition precedent to the seller's loading of the vessel.

The contracts do not refer to anticipatory breaches, which the UCC calls repudiation, and which may give rise to invocations of default. For a default to be found, the injured party must be able to show that it acted in reliance on the repudiation by the other side. A purchaser declaring that the documents will not be lifted may be held in default by the seller. It would be unreasonable to expect delivery to be made when it was clear that payment would not be forthcoming. FOSFA 24 states that a seller may declare "prior to the last day for making a declaration of shipment", that a delivery will not be made, "but the date of that notice shall not become the default date without the agreement of the Buyer". The seller is thus prevented from selecting a date on which the market value would make for the lowest damage liability.

Under a contract for the shipment or delivery of lots in different periods of time, the repudiation of one of these may not involve the others. For instance, GAFTA 30 reads, "each shipment shall be considered a separate contract". If the buyer is in default as to the first lot, prior to the commencement of the shipment period, and the seller acts in accordance with this declaration, there has been an anticipatory breach, which, however, may not apply to the other lots.

A default declaration restores the injured party, as nearly as possible, to the position it would have occupied had the default not occurred. The injured party may effect a transaction at market, to substitute for the one which the other party will not fulfil, and the loss (if any) suffered by covering-in may be claimed against the defaulting party. Usually, by the time the replacement trade can be made, the original delivery period has passed and the new transaction will necessarily bear subsequent dates of performance; but the various conditions should, wherever possible, be the same as those of the defaulted trade. The replacement transaction should preferably be made through a broker and be widely advertised so that the most favourable price is obtained. There is not, as commonly believed, a *duty* of the injured party to mitigate damages. However, if reasonable action to this end is not undertaken (provided it can be done without excessive risk or expense), then the recoverable damages are reduced accordingly.

It may be burdensome for the injured party to make an actual replacement purchase or sale, and the contracts allow, as an alternative, for damages to be computed by the simple use of the market price on the date of default (or, in NAEGA 2, on the tenth day after the default declaration). Under the premise that a defaulter may not gain from its own non-performance, the injured party is allowed to retain a profit—if there is one—resulting from the difference between the contract and market prices. Actually, a gain of this type seldom exists, as it entails for the defaulter the loss of a cheap purchase relative to market levels at the time of default.

Establishing a market value for purposes of fixing damages may be a difficult task if, at the time of default, there is only sporadic trading or no trading at all, in the commodity. It may be necessary to calculate with prices of another market, making adjustments for freight rates, other expenses, quality differences, etc., in order to bring the prices to the required basis.

If the default is caused by the buyer, NAEGA 2 calls for the contract price to be increased by carrying charges when computing the damages. GAFTA and FOSFA contracts provide that if the seller failed to make shipment, the contract price is to be decreased by the extension allowance. Interest may be claimed on the damages accruing from the date of default, but GAFTA 27 and 30 do not allow the buyer recovery of any damages "in respect of loss of profit upon any Sub-Contracts made by themselves or others unless the Arbitrators or Board of Appeal, having regard to any special circumstances, shall in their sole and absolute discretion award such damages". FOSFA 24 excludes all damages other than the difference between the contract price and the market value (as determined by a replacement transaction or by computing the known market value), but it also makes provision for the panel's discretion "if the circumstances of the default justify it".

We have seen that the injured party in a default may claim damages if a loss is sustained. Any gain in the difference between contract and market prices may be retained, and need not be turned over to the defaulter: a party ought not to benefit from its failure to perform. Were the rule otherwise, a party could simply declare itself in default when the market turned in its favour, and reap the benefit, without making any effort to fulfil its obligations.

GAFTA and FOSFA contracts have clauses providing that in the event of insolvency or bankruptcy, the contract shall immediately be closed out by repurchase or resale at market. Any loss in so doing may be claimed from the other party, but any gain is to be turned over to it, contrary to the rule for ordinary defaults. Clause 23 of NAEGA 2 ("Insolvency") provides that a contract may be terminated if a party "suspends payment or commits an act of bankruptcy". If there are "reasonable grounds for insecurity" regarding a party's "financial capacity to perform", a written demand for adequate assurance of performance may be made which, if not met within five days, entitles one to deem the contract terminated.

Certain types of *force majeure* either excuse a party from performance totally or grant it a delay for performance. *Force majeure* occurrences specified by the contracts include actions of government, strikes, lockouts, boycotts, and civil commotion. Detailed treatment is accorded to prohibitions of export and strikes. Prohibition of exports and acts of government in the country of origin of the goods, or the territory where they are situated, give rise to cancellation of the contract in whole or in part, without penalty to either party.

A sale of U.S. wheat c. and f. Turkish ports called for payment under a letter of credit confirmed by a West European or U.S. bank. The buyer, a Turkish government agency, defaulted on the contract, alleging that Turkish law prohibited it from opening the credit. The matter went to original and appeal arbitration in GAFTA, and was referred to the tribunals; the Court of Appeal ruled that since the letter of credit was to be confirmed outside Turkey, the illegality or impossibility claimed by the buyer was not a valid excuse: "[T]he sellers are not in the least concerned as to the method by which the Turkish buyers are to provide . . . the letter of credit."[8]

The prohibition clauses of GAFTA and FOSFA contracts were severely tested by the U.S. Government's 1973 embargo on exports of soyabeans, soyabean meal and other agricultural products. The contract clauses were geared to total prohibition, but the U.S. Department of Commerce on July 2, 1973, announced a validated licensing system under which shipment of 50% of existing soyabeans sales and 40% of soyabean meal sales would be permitted. The reverberations of this partial embargo in London arbitrations and court cases were to last several years, involving even a judgment by the House of Lords after lower tribunals had issued conflicting decisions. Intricate rules of law emerged, mostly because of the nature of the prohibition, and partly because of the confusion created by GAFTA 100, which was heavily involved, and which had a *force majeure* clause as well as a prohibition clause. One was reminded of the Schleswig-Holstein problem in the nineteenth century, "which bristled with so many complications that Lord Palmerston once declared that only two men besides himself had ever understood it; one was dead, the second was crazy, and he had forgotten it".[9] Nine

[8] *Toprak Mahsulleri Ofisi* v. *Finagrain Compagnie Commerciale Agricole et Financiere S.A.* [1979] 2 Lloyd's Rep. 114.

[9] J. Salwyn Shapiro, *Modern and Contemporary European History* . . . , Ed. James T. Shotwell, New Ed. (New York: Houghton Mifflin Co.; Cambridge: Riverside Press, 1946), p. 238.

years after the embrago went into effect, a few cases were still being litigated. Even though the contracts were amended to prevent awful confusion, one shudders to think of such an embargo being imposed again.

The contracts do not cite acts of God as grounds for non-performance or delay in performance. Yet, if a f.o.b. vessel contract calls for the ship to load at a named port, and all loading facilities there become disabled by a hurricane, the seller would undoubtedly be granted additional time for delivery. Unlike the standard contracts examined here, GAFTA 100 treats acts of God in the same manner as *force majeure* occurrences.

Section 265 of the U.C.C. lays down the rules for frustration occurring after a contract is entered into: "Where . . . a party's principal purpose is substantially frustrated without his fault by the occurrence of an event the non-occurrence of which was a basic assumption on which the contract was made, his remaining duties to render performance are discharged, unless the language or the circumstances indicate the contrary."

A vessel was to be loaded at the Canadian Lakehead shortly before the end of the navigation season on the St. Lawrence Seaway. The official grain inspectors went on a strike which lasted into the close of navigation. Since the goods had by law to be officially inspected, they could not be loaded into the vessel for a period of time lasting until at least the opening of navigation, i.e., months away. The seller would probably, under English and New York State law, be excused from performance, without assessment of damages.

STRIKE CLAUSES

The standard contracts have for decades contained strike clauses, which GAFTA 27 and 30 still call "strike" clauses, but which FOSFA 24 refers to as "Strikes, Etc.". NAEGA 2 has adopted the heading "Strikes or other Causes of Delay in Delivery", and includes "riots, strikes, lockouts, interruptions in or stoppages of the normal course of labour, . . . [e]mbargoes or exceptional impediments to transportation, . . . [a]ction by Federal, State or local government or authority". GAFTA 27 and 30 refer only to "strikes, riots and lockouts", to which FOSFA 24 adds "civil commotion". The Prohibition Clauses of GAFTA, FOSFA and NAEGA comprehend "prohibition of export, blockade or hostilities or . . . any executive or legislative act done by or on behalf of the government of the country of origin or of the territory where the port or ports of shipment . . . is/are situate".

The "strike" clauses address themselves only to occurrences which prevent or delay delivery or shipment by the seller at the port of export, either because the events take place at the port, or because they prevent the forwarding of the goods to the port. The English contracts, also, provide against the eventuality of vessels being unable, as a result of the occurrence, to transit from the Great Lakes to the St. Lawrence River.

A seller desiring the protection of these clauses must notify the buyer in writing, not later than two business days after the last day of the shipment period (GAFTA), one business day (FOSFA), or the later of within two business days after the commencement of the occurrences or within two business days after the commencement of the established delivery period (NAEGA). The NAEGA requirement is more stringent, as the buyer, which must arrange for the ocean freight, should be made aware as soon as reasonably possible that there may be a delay in delivery. All the contracts allow for passage of the notice in string, even after the stipulated deadlines. The notices must state the port or ports from which shipment will be made after resumption of work, and shipment may not be made from another port.

GAFTA 27 and 30 provide relief for the seller only if the occurrence takes place during the last 28 days of the shipment period. If this period is less than 28 days, there is no restriction. FOSFA substitutes 30 days, and NAEGA imposes no limitation.

Under the English contracts, the seller is entitled to as much time to ship as there were days remaining in the shipment period, at the time the occurrence began. For a shipment period of March 1–31, and a strike between March 15 and 20, the seller would have until April 5 to make shipment. (March 20, the date of resumption of work, plus the sixteen days which remained in the shipment period on March 15, when the strike commenced.) If the time left for shipment when the occurrence began was 14 days or less, the seller is allowed 14 days. GAFTA limits the time allowed to a maximum of 28 days; presumably, the strike may last so long that it results in frustration of the contract.

NAEGA 2 exonerates the seller from making delivery while the occurrences last; thereafter, delivery must be made to vessels in proper rotation, failing which the seller is liable for damages during the periods when the "by-passing" takes place, at the demurrage rate stipulated in the charter-party for the ship which is being delayed. Addendum 1 also grants the seller relief from demurrage while the occurrence is taking place, and for an equivalent period of time thereafter; however, the seller cannot, through the operation of this provision, earn despatch.

The seller invoking the strike clauses, must submit, in due course, a certificate issued by the North American Export Grain Association, or by a Chamber of Commerce (FOSFA), to substantiate the occurrence, and its dates of commencement and termination.

MARINE INSURANCE

It is vital that commodities in world trade be covered with marine insurance throughout their movement from the loading elevator to the port of delivery overseas, or the warehouse to which the goods are destined. The goods must obviously be insured even before their arrival at the port of loading, but this is not a matter which need detain us here. In f.o.b. vessel contracts, the coverage is to be taken out by the purchaser, but the seller has an abiding interest in knowing that this has been done, and will do so on its own if necessary, rather than risk difficulties in the collection for the goods if the vessel should be involved in an accident. The seller wants to be certain of receiving payment for the goods loaded, even if the vessel sinks alongside the berth after having lifted part of the cargo. NAEGA 2's insurance clause (Clause 14) reads as follows:

> "Marine and war risk (plus strikes, riots, civil commotions and mine risk) insurance, covering seller's/buyer's interests as they may appear, is to be covered by buyer with first-class approved companies and/or underwriters and to be confirmed by such companies and/or underwriters to seller at least 5 days prior to the expected readiness of the vessel. If this confirmation is not received by seller by such time, seller may place such insurance for buyer's account and at buyer's risk and expense."

To avoid burdensome verification and the possibility of costly oversights, the seller may, if desired, place "loading risk" insurance for its own account, affording protection in case the buyer has not taken out the required policy. The seller will also be covered in the event, for instance, that the clean bills of lading required for presentation to the buyer cannot be obtained because the cargo has been lost in a casualty. If shipping documents are used as collateral for bank loans, the bank may require proof of insurance coverage.

The c. and f./c.i.f. contracts require 102% coverage of the invoice value. The basic marine insurance coverage is FPA (free of particular average), under GAFTA 27 and 30, on Lloyd's conditions, including war risk and strike risk insurance on the general conditions set down by GAFTA; FOSFA 24 calls for FPA terms, per London Institute of Underwriters' Cargo Clauses, plus war risk and extended strike risk.

FPA covers the total loss of the goods, as in a sinking of the vessel. Also, losses arising from general average, wherein a sacrifice is made, say by jettisoning some of the cargo, so that the entire venture may be saved. All interests share in such a loss, which is incurred for the welfare of all; for example, the vessel will be required to share *pro rata* in the loss of cargo. Corn on board the vessel may be assessed for the loss of other cargo sacrificed. FPA also covers loss of goods carried, occurring after a casualty. FPA English terms afford recovery whether or not the loss was occasioned by the casualty, or, in other words, whether or not the casualty was the proximate cause of the loss. FPA American terms limit recovery to instances where the casualty *was* the proximate cause of the loss.

Broader cover may be taken out, by agreement of the parties. WA, also known as WPA (with average or with particular average), goes beyond FPA, and includes damage to the cargo caused by sea-water entering the hold in a storm, etc. Like FPA, this policy excludes pilferage, grain going out of condition because of a bulkhead (wall) next to the engine room becoming overheated, grain acquiring an objectionable odour from other cargo, etc.

All-risk insurance, despite its name, does not include damage to the cargo arising from inherent vice, i.e., the natural propensity of organic matter to deteriorate or acquire commercially objectionable characteristics, without the intervention of outside agencies. Rye terms coverage is available, reimbursing the seller for penalties payable to the buyer when the condition of the grain on arrival does not meet the contractual guarantee. The House of Lords upheld the assured's right to claim recovery under a "HSSC" (Heat, sweating and spontaneous combustion) policy.[10] The soyabeans covered had a

[10] *Soya G.m.b.H. Mainz Kommanditgesellschaft* v. *White* [1983] 1 Lloyd's Rep. 122.

moisture content such as to entail a risk, but not a certainty, of deterioration during the voyage.

Costs and expenses occasioned by delays to the vessel are not covered by the standard policies, nor is normal shrinkage in weights en route, for bulk commodities. However, full outturn guarantee may be covered with a superintending firm. Late arrival insurance is available to protect the seller which has guaranteed the arrival of the vessel by a given date, provided the causes are not covered by the usual insurance policy. Steamer name insurance compensates a seller obligated to deliver the goods on a given ship, which sinks before it can perform, etc.

CHAPTER 5

Ocean Freight

Ocean freight is very important to the trading of grain in world markets and to the fulfilment of commodity sales. In examining the distinctions between f.o.b. contracts on one hand, and c. and f./c.i.f. contracts on the other, (see pages 22–25) we have stated that one of the tools of the trader is the chartering of ocean freight; this may also be an aid to the exporter's logistics.

There are market risks associated with "going long" or "going short" ocean freight, since the rates fluctuate, sometimes considerably. It is usually possible to obtain a refusal from a vessel owner for voyages between active ports, e.g., U.S. Gulf to Rotterdam. A refusal is a firm offer made by a vessel owner, normally through a broker, valid for a specified time, e.g., twenty-four hours, to supply a vessel arriving at the port(s) of loading within certain dates, for the carriage of stated commodities to a port or ports, at specified rates of freight, cadence of loading and discharge, and rate of demurrage/despatch. With this refusal in hand, the commodity offer on a c. and f./c.i.f. basis may be calculated. If a sale results, the vessel owner's refusal may become a firm contract, without market risk on the seller's part as to the freight. If the destination is too exotic, it may be difficult to obtain a refusal.

The seller may prefer to treat the ocean freight as a commodity similar to grain, but doing this requires specialised knowledge. Many factors influence freight markets, such as the amount of coal, steel, fertilisers and other commodities presently and prospectively moving in international commerce, the outlook for the supply and demand of grain and oilseeds, the rate of new construction of vessels (or, in current depressed circumstances, the rate of scrapping!), the types of vessels being built, etc. An important difference between grain and ocean freight is that, for the latter, there is no futures market, although it is possible to use refusals and to hedge in some degree by chartering and reletting vessels on highly-travelled routes. Time-charters are of particular interest because of their relative flexibility as to ports of loading and discharge.

Booking ocean freight means hiring a vessel, or space in a vessel. A liner vessel is one engaged in the transportation of goods over a scheduled route. Decades ago, grain was carried by liners such as Cunard passenger vessels loading in the port of New York, but almost all grain in world commerce today is moved by tramp vessels. An occasional parcel of oilseeds (a quantity less than a full cargo) may be shipped by liner under a contract called a booking or engagement note. Conditions of carriage for liners are shown in the bill of lading; the contract of affreightment for these vessels, styled engagement note, does not contain the detailed terms one finds in a charter-party.

"Tramp" is the inelegant expression for a vessel which is not a liner. Freight for these vessels is traded on the floor of the Baltic Exchange in London, and through brokers in New York and several other commercial centres in the world. An agreement to charter (hire) a vessel is called a fixture, and the formal contract between the vessel owner (or, simply, the owner) and the charterer is called a charter-party. Just as there are strings of contracts in the trading of grain, there may be several contracts of affreightment for the same voyage or time charter. A, the owner, has entered into a charter with B, and B with C: as between B and C, B is called the desponent owner.

Two main types of charter are used in the transport of grain. The voyage charter commits the owner to provide a vessel for a given voyage. The ship is made available to the charterer with all necessities, including crew, bunkers, etc., and it must be ready for loading within certain dates. Payment of the freight is made upon completion of loading of the vessel (freight prepaid) or upon arrival at the port of discharge (freight collect). The vessel may be named in the charter, or it may be TBN, i.e., to be nominated prior to arrival at the port of loading. In a consecutive voyage charter, the owner supplies the charterer with a ship for several successive journeys.

A time charter involves the hiring of a ship for a specified period of time, the owner providing the crew and other necessaries, except that the charterer must pay for bunkers (fuel), water, the expenses of piloting, lights, port and other dues. Hire is paid monthly or semi-monthly. The places where the ship is to be delivered to the charterer and redelivered to the owner are specified. Between these dates, the vessel is said to be on hire, and may make such voyages as the charterer chooses, which are not prohibited by the charter-party or by law.

The bareboat or demise charter is similar to the time charter, except that the charterer must provide crew, stores, etc.

When freight is chartered for the performance of a commodity sale, the terms of the charter-party must not conflict with those of the commodity agreement, as this might jeopardise the performance of one or both. The major points to be considered in the chartering of a vessel are:

Type of vessel

The type of vessel best adapted for loading bulk grain from the United States and Canada is the self-trimming bulk carrier. This vessel accommodates the pouring of grain into the holds so that little or no trimming is necessary. The National Cargo Bureau has nonetheless required some trimming even of these ships. Trimming, which causes a slowdown in loading, consists of levelling the grain in the hold so that it will not shift and result in listing. Some vessels are equipped with so-called bleeding tanks, which allow the grain automatically to pour through to a contiguous hold. Loading is more time-consuming with "tweendeckers", where trimming is required as a matter of course, and with tankers, which have small hatch openings. The physical characteristics of the ship are also important in determining at which ports a vessel may load or discharge, and whether lightening (off-loading a portion of the cargo into lighters, before the ship goes into a berth) will be necessary. The draught of the vessel has to do with the amount of water required for the vessel to navigate without touching bottom. Confusion arises from the term "draught", which may be used to specify the charterer's obligation to nominate a port or ports with a certain minimum draught or the owner's obligation to provide a vessel with a stated maximum draught. In commodity sales, these obligations may be assumed respectively by the buyer or by the seller. The ship's length overall (LOA) will determine whether a vessel can be accommodated at a given berth. Beam (width of the ship) and air draught (distance between water line and hatch coaming) will govern whether a ship can be loaded at certain elevators, with or without special arrangements such as shifting the vessel, ballasting, etc. So-called Panamax vessels have physical dimensions permitting them to pass through the Panama Canal. Ore/bulk/oil (Obo) vessels, as is evident from their name, are versatile carriers.

Commodity

One commodity may be specified, or the charterer may have the option of loading two, or more. Heavy grains include wheat, corn, grain, sorghums, rye and soyabeans. Light grains are barley and oats. A ton of corn occupies fewer cubic feet in a vessel's hold than a ton of oats. The freight rate, expressed in dollars per long or metric ton, will be greater for oats than for corn, thus affording the owner roughly the same return for either of the commodities.

Quantity

There is usually a loading tolerance at the option of the vessel, for proper stowage of the cargo.

Laydays/cancelling

The vessel is required, in a voyage charter, to be ready to take on the cargo at the port of loading, at any time between the first date of the laydays, and the cancelling date. If the vessel does not tender notice of readiness within the required period, the charterer may, at its option, cancel the charter when the ship does arrive at the port of loading.

Loading and discharge ports

The charter-party will stipulate these ports, frequently as a range, e.g., Mississippi River ports, USNH (United States North of Hatteras), Antwerp/Hamburg Range, etc., from which the charterer may select one port. The charter may provide that if more than one is selected, the freight rate is increased.

Freight rate

The rate per long or per metric ton is shown in the charter-party. Freight may also be booked on a lump-sum basis, i.e., for an agreed sum of money, regardless of the quantity of cargo loaded.

Laytime

Idle time incurred while the vessel awaits loading or discharge is an expense to the owner; the charter stipulates the amount of time granted the charterer for these operations, once the ship is ready. If it takes longer than this time to load or discharge the cargo, the charterer pays the owner demurrage. If the work is accomplished faster, the owner pays the charterer despatch, traditionally at half the demurrage rate. Demurrage/despatch rates also appear in commodity contracts, i.e., in loading and in discharge rate guarantees, where they tend to reflect the rates in voyage charters; for any given shipment, the cadence of loading and the demurrage/despatch rates may differ as between the commodity contract and the charter-party.

The important factors in calculating demurrage/despatch are:

Time allowed

The charter-party specifies the time allowed the charterer for loading and discharging the commodity, typically a number of tons per day, e.g., 5,000 long tons per weather working day, Sundays and holidays excepted. If the vessel lifts 25,000 long tons, the charterer is allowed five days in which to effect the loading. Laytime commences as stipulated in the charter-party, and runs through to the completion of loading. It consists of time allowed and of time on demurrage thereafter. Completion of loading prior to the expiration of time allowed entitles the charterer to despatch moneys payable by the owner. All-purpose or reversible laydays combine the time for loading with that for discharging.

Commencement of laytime

The charter-party known as Baltimore Form C has provided NAEGA 2 a basic standard for the commencement of laytime in the loading of grain, i.e., on the morning of the working day after the vessel's tender of notice of readiness, whether, at that time, vessel is in berth or only in port, or even only in the roads and thus technically not within the confines of the port. The notice of readiness (N.O.R.) must be given to the charterer or its agent in the port. At loading, the N.O.R. must be accompanied by the ship's "passes", i.e., a stowage certificate issued by the Federal Grain Inspection Service stating that the holds are suitable for loading grain, i.e., that they are not contaminated with previously carried cargo or with insects, as well as a certificate of the National Cargo Bureau stating that the holds have been "prepared in accordance with the regulations of the Commandant of the United States Coast Guard so far as applicable, and with the recommendations of the National Cargo Bureau, Inc.". If a valid stowage certificate cannot be obtained, the holds may have to be cleaned and/or fumigated. The holds of "tweendeckers" may have to be fitted for carrying bulk grain to the satisfaction of the National Cargo Bureau. N.O.R. must be submitted at the port of loading, prior to 4 p.m. on any working day, or by 12 noon on Saturdays. The tendering of the N.O.R. is not an advice to the elevator that the vessel is ready to load; the ship must therefore also file a berth application with the elevator, which is done by the agents for the vessel. The vessel's name is entered into an elevator "line-up", and it awaits its turn to load; meanwhile, it is tied up in anchorage or at a lay berth.

Running of laytime

Grain is usually chartered with a specified tonnage to be loaded per weather working day, Sundays and holidays excepted (WWDSHEX). If the charter contains a loading rate cadence of 5,000 long tons per WWDSHEX, this is understood as an *average* daily rate; if the vessel lifts 25,000 tons, the charterer has five days allowed, or "free" days, in which to load the ship. In reckoning those five days, Sundays and holidays are excluded and Saturdays are treated in accordance with the custom of the port which, in the U.S., means that Saturdays are excepted. It must be emphasised that we are referring to laytime, i.e., time prior to the vessel being on demurrage, having exhausted its "free time". Time is also suspended during periods of rain, snow, etc. WWDSHINC is a rarer alternative to WWDSHEX, and means that time continues to run on Sundays and holidays. WWDSHEX terms may be varied by adding the expression "unless used", meaning that if loading or discharge operations take place, say, on a Sunday, this will not be "free time" to the charterer.

Demurrage

Once the time allowed has expired, the vessel starts on demurrage. From then on, time runs continuously, and there is no exception for Saturdays, Sundays, holidays, time during which there is rain, snow, etc. This is what the expression "once on demurrage always on demurrage" is intended to convey. Time on demurrage multiplied by the daily demurrage rate (say, $4,000 per day or a fraction thereof), yields the sum which the charterer pays the owner.

Despatch

If the loading is completed in less than the time allowed, there is despatch money due by the owner to the charterer. The despatch rate is traditionally half the demurrage rate.

Costs of loading and discharge

The cost of moving the grain from the elevator into the holds of the vessel and the trimming of the grain (if any), are costs to be allocated between the charterer and the owner; the same applies to the costs of discharge. Grain charters are generally made free in and out (F.I.O.), meaning that the expenses of loading and discharge are for account of the charterer, and consequently are *free* to the vessel. If the loading is F.I.O.S.T., then the charterer must also pay the costs of stowing and trimming; it is convenient to remember that the word "free" in these expressions signifies "free to the vessel", i.e. an expense which the vessel does not bear. Liner terms or berth terms mean that expenses of loading and discharge are for account of the owner. A vessel may be chartered with free discharge, i.e., the owner pays costs of loading, but not of discharge.

The grain contracts are interrelated with ocean freight and charter-parties. With regard to shipping, the buyer and the seller assume some of the functions of vessel owner and charterer. In simple terms, under f.o.b. vessel contracts, the seller must provide a loading port (or ports) and berth (or berths) to the vessel within the requirements of the contract; the seller may guarantee a cadence of loading. These functions are also those of a charterer. In c. and f./c.i.f. sales, the roles are reversed, and it is the buyer which must designate the ports and berths of discharge, while the seller's ship must transport the goods thereto. What constitutes proper ports and berths is determined by the contract of sale, taking account of the circumstances. In controverted cases, the matter must be judged by maritime law and usage. For example, if a vessel finds the channel leading to the designated port or berth impossible to navigate because of shallow draught, the liability of buyer and seller, even in a commodity arbitration, must be decided by maritime rules.

The forms of charter-party most widely used in the grain trade are the Approved Baltimore Berth Grain Charter-Party Form C and the North American Grain Charter-Party (Norgrain). The first of these was issued in 1913 as a very short form, touching on what we would consider today to be only a very few points; it is quaint to see a demurrage rate of "four pence British Sterling or its equivalent". In 1963, a much more complete version was issued, approved by the North American Export Grain Association, New York, the North American Shippers' Association, London, and the New York Produce Exchange.[1] Leading owners and charterers seem to have developed their own variations on the Baltimore Form C. Norgrain was introduced in 1973, "recommended by" the North American Export Grain Association, the Baltic and International Maritime Conference, the Chamber of Shipping of the United Kingdom, and the Federation of National Associations of Ship Brokers and Agents. In spite of its distinguished sponsorship, the resulting document did not eclipse the ancient Baltimore Form C, which shows every sign of vigour.

Guarantees of discharge cadences in commodity contracts have existed for several decades, even though they are not mentioned in GAFTA 27 and 30 and FOSFA 24. They are negotiated to conform to the usage and requirements of the destination, and the terms ruling in the ocean freight markets. Inadequate discharge facilities and congested ports caused demurrage to be incurred, which the seller assumed, until the discharge rate guarantee came into being. The purpose of the guarantee is to shift the risk of delays, and the consequent demurrage, to the receiver (or, for f.o.b. vessel sales, to the supplier of the goods), the party presumed to be in control of the discharge (or loading) operations. The seller in c. and f./c.i.f. contracts which collects demurrage from its buyer, also pays demurrage to the vessel owner. In f.o.b. vessel contracts, the buyer collects demurrage from the seller and reimburses the owner. The same principle, turned inside out, applies to despatch. In practice, the guarantees do not give absolute protection to the charterer, for various reasons. The terms of the sales contracts and of the charter-party may differ as to the cadence of discharge (or loading), as to the rate of demurrage/despatch, as to the commencement and counting of laytime, etc. An official buying agency requires the seller to stand

[1] The New York Produce Exchange terminated its commodity and maritime activities in 1973.

demurrage if incurred, but excludes the payment of any despatch. A c. and f./c.i.f. seller, having paid demurrage to the owner, may have difficulty collecting it from buyers, in a very few destinations. Payment for the goods is made upon submission of shipping documents without which the buyer cannot obtain physical possession, but the invoices for demurrage are presented weeks after discharge (or loading), and their prompt payment depends on the *bona fides* of the buyer, backed up by the right to bring arbitration proceedings.

We have stated that rules for *discharge* rate guarantees have not been formalised in the standard contracts. On the other hand, very detailed conditions of a *loading* rate guarantee have appeared in the NAEGA 2 contract since 1978. For example, the rule is set down for calculating demurrage/despatch for goods when the waiting time (time at anchorage or lay berth awaiting an open loading berth) is "shared" with goods delivered against an entirely unrelated contract, either at the same berth, or at different ones. Addendum 1 does not always duplicate charter-party terms. For example, it sets the commencement of laytime on the latest of the following: (1) 0700 hours on the business day after the tender of the notice of readiness and the filing with the elevator, (2) 0700 hours on the business day after expiration of the pre-advice period of vessel nomination, (3) 0000 hours on the first business day of the established delivery period. The laytime under the charter-party would, with Baltimore Form C, commence on the morning of the business day after the tender of the notice of readiness; thus, laytime may commence on one day under the charter-party, and on another under the commodity contract.

As we have said, laytime generally commences as between owner and charterer, on the day following tender of the N.O.R., and charters usually provide that this shall occur, whether the vessel is in berth or not (WIBON), whether in port or not (WIPON), whether customs cleared or not (WCCON), and whether in free pratique or not (WIFPON). All this simply means that the vessel, having arrived at an anchorage, whether within the geographical limits of the port or not, may tender its N.O.R., which alone will trigger the start of laytime. Free pratique refers to the vessel's being cleared by the quarantine authorities. For loading in the United States, the vessel must have obtained its "passes" before tendering N.O.R. The "whether or not" provisions are habitual ones in the grain trade, but not invariable ones, depending on the destinations.

The demurrage/despatch rates in charters are essentially the creatures of supply and demand of ocean freight and, in voyage charters, of the prospects for expeditious (or slow) loading or discharge at the ports involved. In c. and f./c.i.f. contracts to unusual destinations where few transactions are made, the seller will take care to have the charter terms tailored to the sale conditions. In the active markets f.o.b. vessel U.S. ports, the demurrage/despatch rates in the commodity contracts tend to lag behind those of charters.

GAFTA 27 and 30 and FOSFA 24 basically call for discharge in accordance with liner terms in the port(s) of destination, or with custom of the port. NAEGA 2 calls for delivery in accordance with custom of the port "but always subject to elevator tariff". The expression "customary quick despatch" is sometimes used, but it contributes no precision as to what is expected by way of minimum cadence.

As to costs of loading and discharge, these are clearly spelled out in the standard forms. The English contracts stipulate that discharge costs from the hold to the ship's rail are for seller's account and beyond that point, for buyer's account. Of course, these conditions may be, and are, modified at will by the parties. NAEGA 2 calls for the seller to stand the costs to the end of the loading spout; again, this may be varied so as to include stowage and trimming for account of the seller.

A buyer may find that the strike clause appearing in the contract of purchase f.o.b. vessel may be different from that of the charter-party (usually, though not necessarily, the Centrocon Strike Clause). Discrepancies of this sort may be unavoidable, but one should be aware of their possible consequences. The material points are the occurrences covered, and the relief granted—number of days of extension.

An anecdote illustrates vividly the peril caused by dissimilar terms in a sales contract and a charter-party. Two decades ago a sale was made c.i.f. Liverpool/Birkenhead, with the buyer having to declare in which of these twin ports the vessel was to unload. The seller erroneously chartered a ship for Liverpool only, and it had almost reached its destination when the buyer declared Birkenhead. The seller should have been able readily to correct his mistake in chartering, at little or no expense, but for one fact. Vessels bound for Birkenhead must pass under a low bridge, which can be done only if they are equipped with a collapsible mast; the ship in question did not have a collapsible mast. This otherwise diverting story left the seller in default of contract.

CHAPTER 6

Arbitration

WHAT IS ARBITRATION?

David Van Vort, a veteran of the grain community, fondly recalls how, decades ago, he would be pressed into service by colleagues to give his opinion in a commercial disagreement between members of the trade. Merchants met daily on the floor of the New York Produce Exchange, a solid brick building with romanesque window arches, wood panelling and mosaic floor tiles. Van Vort would be taken to one side by the antagonists and he would be asked to decide who was right, and how much money, if any, was to be paid by the "loser": his opinion was unquestioningly accepted by both sides. The recitation of what had happened to cause the grief must have been given rather swiftly, for the entire session was usually over in about 10 minutes. This is not too surprising, as the few spats which came up were not highly technical, and the amounts at stake were not large. These picturesque doings illustrate several of the characteristics of an arbitration. The adversaries agree to submit their controversy to one or more knowledgeable arbitrators, who will hear and consider the evidence and render a decision (an "award") which the parties agree to abide by. Actual arbitrations are, of course, much less casual than Mr. Van Vort's consultations, but they have the same goal: to afford disputants a forum of experts to weigh the pros and cons of their respective positions, with less formality than a court of law, and with far greater despatch.

Arbitration should not be mistaken for mediation, in which the aim is to get both sides to agree to a settlement by dint of reasoning, moral persuasion or other exercises. Arbitrators, in a very real sense, act as judges, and not as peacemakers or midwives to a settlement. Each party presents evidence along with its version of the controversy and gives what it thinks or hopes are unassailable arguments in its favour. Arbitrators are judges of the facts and of the law; they decide matters of procedure and of substance. In the United States, they wield more power than most judges, as their award is, on its merits, normally beyond judicial challenge. It is not advisable to offend them!

Businessmen prefer arbitration to litigation for the relative speed of disposition, and the relatively lower costs. An experienced party saves on legal expenses when it is represented in arbitrations by its own personnel rather than by counsel.

Arbitrations are usually held long after the controversy has arisen and by then it is generally not justifiable to expect that the facts or circumstances be handled confidentially. If there is, however, a legitimate need to protect any data, the arbitrators will give it their serious consideration, always bearing in mind that the rights of the other party must not be prejudiced. Awards are issued by the New York Society of Maritime Arbitrators in a reasoned form, i.e., with an exposition of the facts, the issues and the thinking by which the arbitrators arrived at their judgment. These awards are regularly published by the Society. The American Arbitration Association, in its administration of NAEGA cases, does not make the records available without the specific consent of the parties. Since the awards are not usually issued in "reasoned" form, publishing them would be of little assistance to anyone seeking enlightenment. The type of confidentiality which may be extended in arbitrations makes them a worthwhile alternative to court action, with its risk of widespread and undesired publicity.

ARBITRATE OR SETTLE?

Parties may drift into arbitrations through simple inertia. It is easier to let matters take their course than to enter into lengthy and difficult negotiations. Both parties, when they are in good faith, are well-advised to reach a settlement, rather than to spend time and effort on hearings and briefs.

The settlement process involves three main steps, each vital to success. First, the "right persons" on each side must be willing to discuss the problem. Sometimes the operating people, motivated to do the best job for their firm, and, after a certain amount of time, hardened in their battle positions, reach a stalemate which can only be broken by those who have not been involved in the dispute. The second stage is that of putting across one's point of view. Both parties must be fair listeners or—considering that they are hardly disinterested—they must hear each other out courteously. The last step is arriving at an accord. A party may be able to convince the other to drop its claim, ending the drama right there. Or the horse-trading may commence.

When each side has developed a profound loathing for the other and dedicates its energies to "getting that so and so", it is time to call a halt to the struggle. The few dollars the parties may contrive to extract from each other by cunning or compulsion are more than offset by the time lost and the extinction of goodwill. Officials who have been "above the battle" and who, preferably, know each other personally, may meet alone or in the presence of the chief operating people involved in the bloodshed. The personal contact in itself seems to have a remarkably soothing effect on disputants; it is a lot easier to write resolute and even indignant telexes than to utter the same thoughts over the telephone. In turn, it is a lot easier for most normal persons to say unkind things over the telephone than over a cocktail at lunch, and many problems can be resolved face to face.

Once relative peace, or at least an armed truce has been established, new problems are less apt to arise. If a controversy cannot be laid peacefully to rest, a *modus operandi* may be agreed to in a friendly spirit, such as an arbitration to settle an unusual dispute or, if possible, to establish a general principle for a recurring problem. The award will not be binding for the future, but it will embody the thinking of impartial and knowledgeable persons, and will be particularly valuable if issued in reasoned form. An arbitration in these circumstances is of benefit to the parties and—one hopes—to the trade at large.

Attempts at amicable settlements should be made wherever there is any chance of success. Bringing a simple technical point to the attention of the other side may cause it to realise that its case is weak and that it should spare itself the trouble of an arbitration, and the frustration of losing the award.

The increased role of brokers has reduced personal contact between traders, making co-operation between them much harder to achieve. The following illustration may show how estrangement can impede the solution of a mere tiff. A dispute arose several years ago between two European companies, both of which had American affiliates. Since a NAEGA 2 contract was involved, one of them asked its New York affiliate to assist in the serving of a demand for arbitration. The case was one of misunderstanding, without ill-will on either side, and it was suggested to the European trader by his New York colleagues that a telephone conversation with the other trader on the Continent would set matters right. He turned down this idea, for the curious reason that he had never spoken to the other chap, and he was not anxious to do so now. The dispute was eventually worked out by the patient intervention of the two New York affiliates. Only in this manner was a foolish arbitration avoided.

Disputes over small amounts may not be worth prosecuting, given the time which must be devoted to the preparation and presentation of a case, the legal fees and other expenses, and the possible loss of goodwill. The grain trade in the United States has restrained itself from unleashing floods of arbitrations, for which it deserves to be commended.

Resorting to arbitration only when one has a solid case will eventually convince others in the trade that, when this remedy *is* invoked, it is best to attempt a settlement. A case of any importance will take the time of traders, of the advocates, of witnesses, and of those supplying documents and information. If claims are small or if chances of success are slim, there may be no reason for going forward; on the other hand, the debtor may be relying precisely on the fact that small amounts do not warrant prosecution. An arbitration will show that one is serious about taking all proper remedies to get one's legitimate bills paid, whether large or small. The structure of rates for foreign exchange, needed to make a payment, may be such as to benefit the procrastinating debtor; and there may be significant differences in interest rates. Some firms can be moved to consider claims against them only by the threat of arbitration; as the day of the hearing draws nearer, they seem to become more accessible to reason. Yet demands for arbitration should be served only when one is ready to follow through if the other side will not come to terms.

Whether to initiate an arbitration against an insolvent party is a legal question, but, obviously, if the amount likely to be recovered is less than the anticipated expenses, the exercise may not be worth undertaking.

The commercial implications of an action should be weighed. One does not act lightly with substantial buyers: They have been compared to the gorilla of whom it was asked, "Where does a 500-lb. specimen of this sort sleep?" Response, "Wherever it likes".

When a seller could not collect amounts due from a Far Eastern buyer, despite the latter's admission that the money was due and owing, the seller initiated an arbitration. A mighty indignation came over the buyer, which threatened to blacklist its bold opponent.

When this action seemed imminent, the seller felt compelled to withdraw the demand for arbitration. The claim was correct and fully justified, but it had to yield to the potential loss of an important client.

Some cultures shun arbitration or litigation as being unseemly; Japanese firms, heavily involved in business with Western companies, no longer avoid these actions as a matter of principle.

Arbitrations can be averted by the careful management of contracts and executions, and the desire to resolve problems amicably. Employees conscientiously defending what they see as the interests of their fim should not be discouraged when they are in the right, but should be made to realise that trivial differences ought not to be nurtured into irremediable conflicts.

STATUS OF PRIVATE SETTLEMENTS

Just as the courts favour arbitration over litigation, arbitrators prefer that disputes be settled amicably, but it is not their role to be involved in negotiations between the parties. Occasionally, they may be asked to incorporate a voluntary agreement in an arbitration award, for the official allocation of foreign exchange needed to pay the award, or for other legal reasons.

Arbitrations are held to resolve disputes, and not to create new ones by taking up for adjudication questions on which both parties agree. If arbitrators meddle in undisputed matters, they are said to be acting *ultra vires*, i.e., outside the scope of their authority. A case involved a claim and a counterclaim, for substantial sums of money. The parties had agreed that the award, whether in favour of the claimant or the respondent, would carry interest from the date of the controversy to the date of adjudication. The panel's award omitted interest and could conceivably have been challenged in court, even though the error was made in good faith.

Proposals for settlement should be in writing and set out as clearly as possible, with the classical formula, "this offer is made without prejudice to any of our legal rights". The purpose of this phrase is to free the offeror from any obligation if the proposal is not accepted.

The offer should set a time limit for the receipt of a reply; if the offer is not accepted, the parties are free to start haggling all over again, to bring the matter to arbitration, or to drop it altogether.

If agreement is reached, it should be formalised in a document signed by both parties, stating in essence that it is in full and final settlement of any and all claims by both parties under the contract. The recourse for non-compliance, presumably arbitration, should be clearly stated. If this is not done, the settlement could be construed as a separate accord, not covered by the arbitration agreement of the original contract, and enforceable only in a court of law.

The stipulation as to when the agreed sum is to be paid is a vital element in arriving at an acceptable settlement amount. Where the other party is basically a good firm suffering a temporary cash squeeze, additional time may be granted; but assurances of payment, preferably by a third party, are advisable.

How does one calculate the figure at which one is willing to settle? Negotiators will give different replies to this question, and most will be unable to articulate their *modus operandi*. Some favour a mathematical formula taking account of the sum one can reasonably assume the arbitrators would award, the percentage chances of "winning", etc. Generally, "arriving at a number" is a more subtle process, in which traits of character weigh heavily, whether consciously or not. As negotiations are exchanges between human beings who are usually possessed of assertive personalities, it may be futile to attempt simple "quantification"; the process, rather, is a mixture of cold evaluation, a very large dose of judgment, and more than a dash of intuition. Beside the merits of the case, one must also weigh the effects of an arbitration on commercial relations with the other side, the advantage of a lesser sum, paid forthwith, and even the possibility that winning an arbitration may put one in an undesirable position in future cases of the same kind. The likelihood that the loser of an award might find legal means to defer payment for a few years may be a compelling reason for agreeing to a smaller amount, without further litigation. It is particularly helpful, in negotiations, of course, to know the bent of mind of one's opposite number: is one dealing with a poker player, one who enjoys lengthy *quid pro quos* . . . ?

Wise advocates will recommend that their client entertain a fair settlement as the best resolution of a dispute. A case was pending before an English court of law, on appeal from an arbitration award. It seems that, quite independently of each other, the attorneys for each litigant suggested to their client that they settle the case rather than continue legal action, as a recent court case had been decided on principles favourable to the other side in the current dispute. Presumably, each of the attorneys was referring to a different court judgment! An amicable settlement was arrived at, with each side feeling it had got the better of the other, in view of its lawyer's advice. They both benefited in that the agreement was fair and saved them from further expenditure of time and money.

THE AGREEMENT TO ARBITRATE

In praising arbitration over litigation, we may have conveyed the idea that these processes are mutually exclusive. The courts do play a role with arbitrations, and the law has a prominent function.

The first question which the courts may be called upon to decide is one awkwardly called arbitrability. The judiciary, both in the United States and in England, is favourably disposed toward recognising and enforcing arbitration agreements. One cannot be made to submit to arbitration in the absence of such an agreement, but if one does exist, it cannot be revoked. In GAFTA, FOSFA and NAEGA contracts, it is contained in the arbitration clauses. If there is no valid contract, there is no agreement to arbitrate and, not surprisingly, such a proceeding cannot be foisted on an unwilling party. In a 1977 case before a Federal court in New York,[1] the question was whether there was an enforceable agreement to arbitrate. The court was asked by the petitioners to stay the arbitration; they contended that there had been no discussion of arbitration during the negotiations leading to the sale of the grain, and that the NAEGA 2 form on which the specific contract terms had been typed bore the signature line on its front, whereas the arbitration clause appeared on the reverse side. The front read "See Conditions and Rules on the other side", but the petitioners (buyers of the grain) maintained that they had no reason, when signing the contract, to examine the reverse of the form; *ergo*, the arbitration agreement was unenforceable under Italian law, which they claimed applied to the transaction. The court was not impressed by this line of argument, and stated: "There is no doubt that the quoted legends on the face of NAEGA 2 are sufficient to give notice to a reasonably prudent person of the arbitration provision and other things appearing on the back." The court refused to stay the arbitration.

[1] *Ferrara S.p.A. and United Grain Growers Ltd., and Fratelli Moretti Cereali S.p.A. and United Grain Growers Ltd.*, 77 Civ. 3549 (MEF) and 77 Civ. 3350 (MEF). U.S. District Court for the Southern District of New York.

Courts are called upon to designate arbitrators when the agreement does not stipulate how they are to be selected, or if two arbitrators cannot agree on the designation of a third one, etc. This function of the court does not arise with the contracts discussed here, for they are clear and specific as to the manner of selection of the panel. They are also unambiguous as to the governing law, whether that of New York State or of England; in cases where there is doubt, the matter must be put to a court for its decision.

INITIATING THE ARBITRATION: "COMMERCIAL PEOPLE"

In GAFTA and FOSFA actions, the claimant designates an arbitrator, and so advises the other party. If the arbitrator declines to serve, a substitute must be named; if the other party does not appoint an arbitrator, the association may do so on its behalf. If the two designees cannot agree on a third one (still called "umpire" in the FOSFA rules), the association may make a nomination. GAFTA permits the parties to agree on a single adjudicator. There are prescribed deadlines for all these actions.

Who may serve as arbitrator? GAFTA stipulates a member or an employee of a member firm of that Association, "engaged or who has been engaged in the trade"; FOSFA requires that the arbitrators or umpires, at the time of appointment, "be nominated to the Federation by a full member, company or firm or [be] persons who are full members of the Federation". Persons who have a direct or indirect financial stake in the outcome of the arbitration may, of course, not serve. It is inadvisable for them to serve if there was an involvement in the transaction in dispute by their firm or employer, whether or not it is actually a party to the arbitration.

Under the Grain Arbitration Rules of the American Arbitration Association ("AAA"), covering disputes arising from NAEGA 2 contracts, the claimant sends a demand for arbitration to the respondent, together with a copy of the particular and standard form contracts. The case and the relief sought are described briefly; all the papers are sent to the Tribunal Administrator of the AAA, with a cheque for its fee. The arbitrators are not appointed by the parties, but serve in alphabetical order from a standing list. This approach is also used, for instance, by the Netherlands Oils, Fats and Oilseeds

Trade Association (NOFOTA). Arbitrators on NAEGA cases are not permitted to discuss any aspect of the case with the parties, except in open hearing, in the presence of the entire panel and of all the parties. They are informed of the "bare bones" of the dispute by the tribunal administrator, as set forth in the claimant's demand, to enable them to judge whether they can accept the appointment. They are sent an oath of office, and make disclosures in writing of any circumstances which might bear on their impartiality. The parties may issue challenges for cause, which are ruled upon by the administrator; the arbitrator may resign, or be upheld, or be disqualified by the administrator.

Commodity arbitrators are experienced in the trade and familiar with its terminology and practices. It would be frustrating and perilous to submit oneself to a panel unable to distinguish between a tender of a notice of appropriation and a tender of a notice of readiness. Courts recognise and appreciate the specialised knowledge possessed by "commercial" people. It was recently stated by a court that a panel could consider evidence submitted by the parties regarding market values, "in the light of its own experience and knowledge which it need not canvass before the parties at the hearing".[2]

Rules of GAFTA, FOSFA and AAA, allow for proceedings to be held, by agreement of the parties, in places other than London and New York, respectively; the option is hardly ever exercised.

BOARDS OF APPEAL

GAFTA and FOSFA awards may be reviewed by Boards of Appeal constituted by the associations. The parties may submit their case orally or in writing, but they may not be represented by attorneys at hearings, unless special permission is obtained. There is no appeal mechanism under the Grain Arbitration Rules administered by the AAA.

CONSOLIDATIONS

A large number of shipments (particularly under f.o.b. vessel terms) involve series of contracts. In strings, parties may receive claims

[2] *F. R. Waring (U.K.) Ltd.* v. *Administraçao Geral do Acucar e do Alcool E.P.* [1983] 1 Lloyd's Rep. 49.

which they pass along in their own name to the next party in line. If a claim is received from one's buyer for demurrage under a loading rate guarantee, it is then asserted against one's seller. Should the disputes end up in separate arbitrations for each contract, there is a possibility that, despite the facts and the issues being the same, one could lose both actions. In any event, duplicate proceedings of this kind cause extra, unnecessary work and expense. If the parties agree, under the Grain Arbitration Rules governing NAEGA contracts, to a consolidated proceeding, the disputes will be heard consecutively by the same panel in the same hearing. Any differences in contract terms or in the relevant facts between each of the contracts will be carefully considered by the arbitrators, so as to maintain what is called "privity of contract". In our example of demurrage, the delivery period in one transaction might be October 1–21, in another, October 12–31; if this were a material difference, it would be taken into account by the arbitrators. Each purchase and sale stands on its own; one's non-performance *vis-à-vis* a buyer is not excused by the insolvency of one's supplier. The panel's award in consolidated proceedings is broken down into separate decisions for each contract.

Consolidated arbitrations arising from contracts of the National Institute of Oilseed Products, administered by the American Arbitration Association in San Francisco, resulted in awards where the last party in a string was directed to pay damages to the first one, skipping over all the others. This approach can be very deleterious: the winner of an award may be unable to collect from a firm with which it never contracted, and with which it might have been unwilling to deal.

If a party objects to a consolidation, United States courts will generally compel it "if the issues [in the several arbitrations] are substantially the same and if no substantial right is prejudiced".[3]

GAFTA and FOSFA rules on consolidation have not been carried as far as those in the United States. GAFTA includes only disputes on quality/condition, where the arbitration "may be held between the first seller and the last buyer in string as though they were contracting parties [with each other]"; all other parties must submit contracts and "all relevant information" to the arbitrators. The award may be reviewed by the Board of Appeal on application of *any* of the parties. Presumably, consolidation of GAFTA cases on technical matters (i.e., other than for quality/condition) can be achieved only by

[3] Martin Domke, *The Law and Practice of Commercial Arbitration* (Mundelein, Ill.: Callaghan and Co., 1968), p. 272.

agreement between the parties. FOSFA rules for technical arbitrations spell out that the agreement of all the parties is required. Any party may take the award before the Board of Appeal, "as though a separate award had been made under each contract". The danger of conflicting awards may be met by parties agreeing that the disputes are to be heard separately but by the same panel, which is unlikely, one trusts, to come up with inconsistent results.

SUPERCONSOLIDATIONS

"Superconsolidation" is the formidable expression we shall use for the hearing in related proceedings of commodity and maritime cases with common issues and facts. An English judge bemoaned "the additional expense of two hearings covering the same ground, and the hearing of the owners' and charterers' claims without either owners or charterers knowing what points might be taken by the *buyer*, without the *buyers* being represented and with no one being bound by the other arbitration".[4] The judge's point is entirely valid, despite the convoluted syntax. An embryonic movement toward consolidations which "cut across" forums may be under way in the United States, bringing relief to the charterer caught between the vessel owner and the commodity buyer or seller. This approach would cure the dilemma of conflicting of demurrage under a charter-party on the one hand, and a commodity agreement on the other. The charterer/seller or buyer has been forced to appear before separate forums, with the attendant risks.

Maritime panels have somewhat alleviated the jeopardy of charterers by awarding them damages once thought to pertain to commodity contracts, and therefore held too remote or consequential for the disputes between owners and charterers. In the *Mary S* arbitration,[5] an owner's actions "constituted a wilful and flagrant breach of the charter-party". The vessel refused to perform, allegedly because of a snowstorm and the likelihood of not loading its cargo prior to the official closing of the Lakes. The ship was then chartered on a "spot" basis for loading at a port *further west*. The charterer brought an

[4] *Maritime Transport Operators G.m.b.H.* v. *Louis Dreyfus et Cie; Dreyfus* v. *Société Commerciale de Cereales et Financière S.A.; Soc. Com.* v. *Andre et Cie* [1981] 2 Lloyd's Rep. 161.

[5] New York Society of Maritime Arbitrators, No. 1355.

arbitration to recover, *inter alia*, carrying charges assessed by the supplier, the Canadian Wheat Board, for winter storage costs on the commodity which the vessel had not lifted. The panel held that the owner was responsible for the charges which, though not mentioned in the charter-party, were the "natural and foreseeable consequences of the Owner's actions".

There have been other, similar, awards in New York and in London, but, to the writer's knowledge, the first step toward superconsolidations was taken in February 1983 by the U.S. District Court for the Southern District of New York.[6] It was ordered that the proceeding held to determine the commodity issue between buyer and seller should be attended also by the maritime panel, which would gain a valuable insight for its own subsequent adjudication. Whether superconsolidations are a wave of the future is a matter of fascinating speculation.

TIME-BARS

Courts of law may be involved where delays in bringing arbitration may be so protracted as to cause inequities to the respondent, or where stipulated deadlines would be unreasonably short under the particular circumstances. In England, a number of suits have been brought lately on questions of delay, not only in initiating arbitrations but in their prosecution, that is, in actually going forward with the case.

NAEGA 2 does not have a limitation as to the time by which a demand for arbitration must be served. The question whether an action is time-barred can be a vexed one. Domke says that "[t]he effect of the statute of limitations on arbitration presents a complex problem especially as to its character as substantive or procedural law".[7] An attempt to apply a four-year statute of limitations under New York State law failed before an authoritative federal court.[8] The tribunal upheld the U.S. District Court: this being a procedural and not a substantive question, federal law applied, and not that of New York State. It had been in the arbitrators' discretion not to apply the time-bar.

[6] 82 Civ. 2886 CSH.
[7] Domke, p. 185.
[8] In a case not officially reported.

GAFTA and FOSFA contracts are specific on the deadlines for nominating an arbitrator; the time limits are more stringent for quality/condition disputes than for technical ones. The former require examination of samples, which may be subject to changes over a period of time, through the action of atmospheric moisture, temperature, etc.

The English contracts recite that if the deadlines are not met for commencing an arbitration, i.e., by nomination of an arbitrator, "the claim shall be deemed to be waived and absolutely barred unless the arbitrators . . . or Board of Appeals shall in their absolute discretion, otherwise determine". If the claim is held time-barred, it will not be heard on its merits in a court of law, as this would be a simple means of circumventing the arbitration agreement. Courts do rule on time-bars: "[a] clause barring a claim if arbitration is not commenced within a certain time is not absolute in effect: the court has power to extend the time fixed (notwithstanding that it has already expired) if 'undue hardship' would otherwise be caused."[9] The issue of delay in prosecuting the action, after the arbitrators have been named, was dealt with by the House of Lords in *The Hannah Blumenthal.*[10] The arbitration agreement was held to be a contract separate from the underlying one; it can be terminated by the parties legally abandoning or frustrating it.

A bizarre time-bar can be found in the Vegetable Oil Rules—Export Contract of the American Fats and Oils Association, Inc., requiring that the demand for arbitration be made "within thirty calendar days after vessel carrying the material has arrived in its port of discharge, otherwise the provisions of [the arbitration agreement] shall be deemed waived by the parties". This clause seems to disregard the possibility of the goods never being placed on board a vessel, or of a vessel meeting with a casualty during the ocean voyage. Also, the 30-day period is unreasonably short for claims of demurrage at destination, where the vessel may be forced to wait that long before even being called into berth to discharge.

[9] Anthony Walton, Q.C., *Russell on the Law of Arbitration* (London: Stevens & Sons, Ltd., 1970), p. 61.

[10] *The Hannah Blumenthal* [1983] 1 Lloyd's Rep. 103.

ARBITRATION AND THE LAW

The courts also oversee arbitrations, as guardians of the parties' right to impartial and proper conduct of the proceedings. The United States Arbitration Act[11] gives the following grounds for vacating awards:

(a) Where the award was procured by corruption, fraud, or undue means.
(b) Where there was evident partiality or corruption in the arbitrators, or either of them.
(c) Where the arbitrators were guilty of misconduct in refusing to postpone the hearing, upon sufficient cause shown, or in refusing to hear evidence pertinent and material to the controversy; or of any other misbehaviour by which the rights of any party have been prejudiced.
(d) Where the arbitrators exceeded their powers, or so imperfectly executed them that a mutual, final and definite award upon the subject-matter submitted was not made.

Paragraph (d) of the U.S. statute opens the award to challenge if the arbitrators have exceeded their powers. To take a fictitious example, a dispute involving only demurrage under a loading rate guarantee: if carrying charges were paid and never contested, the arbitrators would be misconducting themselves if they ruled that the charges should be refunded.

The court may, in vacating the award, direct that the arbitrators rehear the case. The New York State Arbitration Law[12] lists substantially the same grounds for vacating as the federal statute.

Arbitrations of NAEGA contracts take place in oral hearings, unless the parties agree to written submissions only. The parties are in attendance by right and may be represented by counsel in all phases of the arbitration. In original GAFTA and FOSFA actions, the parties may be present at the hearings, but they must give advance notice. Attorneys are barred who are "wholly or principally engaged in private practice" (GAFTA); FOSFA is a bit more stringent, excluding "Counsel, solicitor or any members of the legal profession". The same provisions apply to the respective Boards of Appeal, except that the Boards have the discretion to waive them.

[11] Title 9, U.S. Code, §§1–14.
[12] Article 75, C.P.L.R.

An award may be vacated because of the failure of arbitrators to disclose material facts about themselves which could bear upon their impartiality, such as having a personal interest in the outcome of the case. Disclosure may result in a challenge to the arbitrator. In some forums, such as the New York Society of Maritime Arbitrators, the arbitrators will decide whether to disqualify themselves and step down, or to remain on the case. In grain cases, the American Arbitration Association has final authority on the question of disqualification, except of course, for subsequent review by the courts.

Arbitrators may be guilty of misconduct if they do not follow the basic procedures which are recognised as securing the legal rights of the parties. For example, they must make all the evidence submitted to them by one party available to the other.

English arbitrators must observe basically the same legal safeguards as their American counterparts.

We have said that the law plays a significant part in arbitrations; NAEGA requires the panels to apply New York State law, and GAFTA and FOSFA, English law. This is not a matter to be taken lightly: it is an obligation of the panels, even though they are not held to the rigorousness expected of a jurisprudent. In fact, an award will not necessarily be set aside if the panel has misconstrued the law.

An English judge, Mr. Justice Donaldson, whimsically said, "A foreign lawyer—or indeed a native layman—must find the English law on arbitration very odd. If you pause to consider it . . . it *is* very odd. Arbitrators, like Judges, can get the facts wrong. They can get the law wrong. On occasion, given a little ill luck, they can get both wrong."[13]

For oral hearings, rules of procedure are far less ritualistic than in a court of law, but each side's basic rights must be protected. Thus, the claimant is heard first, so that the respondent may know the items of claim, and the arguments advanced against it, before rebuttal.

An arbitration may go forward in the absence of one of the parties; it is then called *ex-parte*. To succeed, the case must be proved against the non-participating side, on the preponderance of evidence, just as if both contenders were present. The written record of the proceedings, if there is one, must be sent to the missing party, together with the evidence and the briefs submitted to the panel. Notice must be given in advance of any hearings.

[13] *Tramountana Armadora S.A.* v. *Atlantic Shipping Co. S.A.* [1978] 1 Lloyd's Rep. 393.

The substantive law which the arbitrators must apply affects, of course, the determination of the case on its merits. It is established that a clause which has been typed in takes precedence over the printed text in which it appears; that an unclear clause may be construed against the party which drafted it. These are principles which govern as a matter of course. Frequently, in weighing the merits of a case, arbitrators may apply a demonstrated custom of the trade, which has full force of law. Fundamental questions of law may be put to a panel: is a buyer justified in claiming that a contract cannot be enforced because the authorities in the country of destination refuse to make the foreign exchange allocation necessary to effect the payment which the contract requires to be made in the seller's country? Statutes and international accords may be cited to the panel by the advocates. The arbitrators are quite capable of following the submissions of each side, and of arriving at an award based on the law. In our example, the answer has been to hold the buyer to the contract: there was no impediment to making the payment required under the contract, since the exchange regulations did not bear on the performance of the buyer, obligated to effect payment *in the seller's country*.[14]

The right of due process, i.e., the right "to have one's day in court", is fundamental to Anglo-Saxon jurisprudence. In England, on questions of substance, court review could be obtained readily prior to the Arbitration Act of 1979, which has greatly curtailed the right of appeal to the judiciary.

FINALITY OF AWARDS

The finality of arbitration awards was laid down by the U.S. District Court for the Southern District of New York in the 1953 case of *Wilko* v. *Swan*.[15] The doctrine of "manifest disregard of the law" was enunciated as the grounds on which an award may be vacated on its merits. This principle of law has since been interpreted by federal courts as requiring, in order to vacate the award, more than "mere error in the law or failure on the part of the arbitrators to understand or apply the law"; the challenge may succeed if it is shown that the

[14] *Toprak Mahsulleri Ofisi* v. *Finagrain Compagnie Commerciale, Agricole et Financière, S.A.* [1979] 2 Lloyd's Rep. 98.

[15] 346 U.S. 427.

arbitrators "deliberately disregarded what they knew to be the law in order to reach the result they did".[16]

No arbitration award was overturned on a finding of "manifest disregard of the law", until 1983, when the U.S. District Court for the Southern District of New York vacated an award which "in effect, directed respondent to violate [a] Dutch decree." (83 Civ. 1485 [KTD]).

The English Parliament recognised, with the Arbitration Act of 1979, the necessity of restricting court review. Cases on appeal to the judiciary were proliferating, arbitration had almost become a mere first round in the adjudication of disputes, and several years went by before final disposition of the cases. There was talk that London could not remain the leading home for international arbitrations unless the system was reformed. The Arbitration Act has not put an end to judicial review: it has made it more difficult to obtain. Nevertheless, the Act effectively prevents the parties from simply "contracting out" of the right to appeal to courts on substantive questions, under GAFTA and FOSFA contracts.

The House of Lords in *The Nema* case,[17] laid down the principles for interpreting the Act. For leave to appeal generally, it is necessary to show "either (i) that the arbitrator misdirected himself in point of law or (ii) that the decision was such that no reasonable arbitrator could reach". Lord Diplock then differentiated between cases with "one-off" clauses, and those with standard clauses. One-off terms are expressions not previously used and that have no established meaning "of which each party was entitled to assume the other knew when he entered the contract, but [are] also unlikely to be used in future by any other parties". The criteria for allowing court review of "one-off" cases are strict: "leave [to appeal] should not normally be given unless it is apparent to the judge upon a mere perusal of the reasoned award itself without the benefit of adversorial argument, that the meaning ascribed to the clause by the arbitrator is obviously wrong."

Access to the courts on the merits of an award is more liberal where the interests of the trade at large are engaged, and where legal construction of a vexed point may be of considerable assistance in the future: "If the decision of the question of construction in the

[16] U.S. District Court for the Southern District of New York, 82 Civ. 1302 (PNL); cited in *The Arbitrator*, New York Society of Maritime Arbitrators, Inc., Vol. 14, No. 2 (Nov. 1982).

[17] *Pioneer Shipping Ltd. and Others* v. *B.T.P. Tioxide Ltd.* [1981] 2 Lloyd's Rep. 239.

circumstances of the particular case could add significantly to the clarity and certainty of English commercial law it would be proper to give leave [to appeal] in a case sufficiently substantial to escape the ban imposed by the first part of section 1(4) [of the Arbitration Act 1979]." This section does not permit leave to be given unless the High Court considers that, having regard to all the circumstances, the determination of the question of law concerned could substantially affect the rights of one or more of the parties to the arbitration agreement.

The recent English developments have served markedly to decrease judicial appeals. One wonders whether, in the catastrophic Embargo of 1973, true finality of awards—with no access to the courts—could have created legal principles of broad application for subsequent actions.

Whether the American or the English system is superior, is a matter of perennial and—mostly—good-natured debate across the Atlantic. In fairness to the English, one must bear in mind that the courts reviewing arbitration awards deal in commercial matters only—a considerable advantage in understanding the facts and deciding the issues. The judges are experienced in dealing with charter-parties, grain contracts, letters of credit, etc. The venerable Lord Justice Denning departed from judicial aloofness in his remarks on the House of Lords overturning a judgment of his Court of Appeal: "Now we have to face the fact that the House of Lords reversed our decision in *Bremer Vulkan Schiffbau und Maschinenfabrik* v. *South India Shipping Corporation* . . . They did so in terms which have given everybody an infinity of trouble ever since."[18]

The biggest drawback to the American system is that arbitrations do not create binding precedent and conflicting awards may be rendered without the practical possibility of appeal.

In 1978, there were held in New York two separate maritime arbitrations on the same questions, viz., whether, under the Exxonvoy 1969 form of charter-party, the charterer could amend the port of discharge. In the first arbitration it was decided that the charterer had no right to do this. The second award was rendered several months later and held just the opposite.[19] There was effectively no legal remedy for this curious divergence. Had the arbitration been held in London with English law to govern, an appeal to the courts might

[18] *The Argonaut* [1982] 2 Lloyd's Rep. 214, at p. 218.
[19] *The Arbitrator*, Vol. 11, No. 2 (January 1979).

have been possible; their decision would then carry the weight of precedent, giving the trade clear rules.

If the aim of arbitration is promptness of adjudication, then finality of the award is almost a necessity. But finality *per se* is not enough, for arbitrations of NAEGA contracts take several months to dispose of, even in relatively simple cases.

On the Continent, it is not unusual for arbitrators to favour an equitable approach over a legal one. A Dutch commentator, Robert van Delden, attributes the existence of English legal review to the panels having to be governed by legal concepts.[20] It logically follows that courts oversee the proper application of juridical precepts; they would consider a "fair" businessman's reasoning as beyond their scope.

Mr. van Delden writes that it took five tribunals (aside from the original panel) to come to a final determination of the tolerance applicable to damages in cases of buyer's defaults.[21] The adjudication by the House of Lords took place in February 1981, the dispute having begun in mid-1975. During these years, the trade was left in suspense as to a basic issue. On the other hand, once the principle was laid down, it applied uniformly, and could not be disregarded by a panel bent on meting out its own justice.

The ideal might be to have judicial review only on questions vital to the trade at large, and to obtain final decisions promptly. The English have restricted access to tribunals, but they have not come to grips with the inordinate delays which characterise all legal systems. Expeditious disposal of cases along the judicial ladder would require profound changes in tradition, attitudes, and procedures. But such efforts might be worthwhile.

The international nature of arbitration makes it necessary to draw on the best ideas of all those in the field; this is not simply an English, or an American, or a Continental question.

[20] Robert van Delden, "English Commodity Arbitrations: A Foreigner looking around in London", in *The Art of Arbitration, Essays on International Arbitration, Liber Amicorum Pieter Sanders* . . . , ed. J. C. Schultsz and A. J. van den Berg (Deventer: Kluwer Law & Taxation Publishers, 1982), p. 97.

[21] *Ibid.*, p. 97, n. 4.

ENFORCEMENT OF AWARDS

Most firms honour arbitration awards as the outcome of a process to which they subscribed by contract. Losers may not agree with the award, but very few complain in good faith that they were dealt with unfairly. There is a general acknowledgment that arbitration is a salutary and relatively efficient way to handle disagreements and that to weaken it is harmful to all. GAFTA and FOSFA release lists of "defaulters" on arbitration awards, i.e., firms which do not pay the amounts adjudicated. These Associations satisfy themselves that there is no valid excuse for the non-payment, such as foreign exchange regulations; the "defaulter" is given every opportunity to vindicate its position before being placed on the list. The system is thought to be a strong incentive to comply with awards, except perhaps for those firms which do not intend to remain active in the trade.

As we have seen, many legal challenges to awards may be made, and once these have run their course, it is yet possible to delay the effect of arbitral judgments, simply by withholding payment. The winner, discouraged by the obstacles in collecting, may become amenable to a settlement, or the loser may be in a temporary cash "bind" which it hopes time will cure. If there is procrastination, it is up to the other side to assert its rights. It may be possible to attach the loser's foreign assets in satisfaction of the award, or an enforcement action may be required in courts of the non-payer's country. The latter can be a frustrating endeavour if these tribunals are hostile to arbitration *per se*; also, legal arguments may be interposed there which might not be valid under the law applicable to the contract.

The 1958 United Nations Convention on the Recognition and Enforcement of Foreign Arbitral Awards, also known as the New York Arbitration Convention, has aided in the enforcement of awards. In 1981, there were almost 60 contracting states[22].

The essence of the Convention is in Article III:

> "Each Contracting State shall recognise arbitral awards as binding and enforce them in accordance with the rules of procedure of the territory where the awards are relied upon, under the conditions laid down in the following articles. There shall not be imposed substantially more onerous conditions or higher fees or charges on the recognition or enforcement of arbitral awards to which this Convention applies than are imposed in the recognition or enforcement of domestic arbitral awards."

[22] Albert J. van den Berg, "Should an international arbitrator apply the New York Arbitration Convention of 1958?", in *The Art of Arbitration*, *op. cit.*, n. 20, p. 39.

Recognition and enforcement may be refused in the country where sought for various reasons, including that "the subject-matter of the difference is not capable of settlement by arbitration under the laws" of the said country (Article IV, 2(a)), or that recognition or enforcement would be contrary to its public policy (Article IV, 2(b)). In some jurisdictions, the award must be reasoned in order to have legal standing in the courts. On the other hand, an Italian jurisprudent writes that "[u]nder French or Italian laws, for example, a domestic award, rendered, let us say, in England where no reasons need be given, may however be enforced in France and Italy".[23]

"Public policy" has been referred to as embodying "an overriding interest of society",[24] but the expression is subject to differing national interpretations; it is less likely to be successfully invoked in international cases than in domestic ones. Public policy is, at all events, one of the means by which the award may be reviewed on its merits by a court in the loser's country. This may frustrate the Convention's aim of having the award stand in foreign courts, without a hearing *de novo* on substantive issues.

Despite the advantages of the New York Convention, enforcement can be cumbersome, time-consuming and costly. Some jurisdictions may not sanction payment of interest on an award when it is affirmed; enforcement is certain to involve legal expense. An award rendered by FOSFA may take a couple of years to enforce in India, for instance, even though that nation is signatory to the Convention.

The picture, though, is not as bleak as may be imagined, since most disputes are resolved short of arbitration, and most awards are honoured as a matter of course.

[23] Giorgio Bernini, "The enforcement of foreign arbitral awards by national judiciaries . . .", in *The Art of Arbitration op. cit.*, n. 20., p. 59.

[24] *Restatement, Second*, "Contracts", 2d., Vol. 2, p. 2.

CHAPTER 7

Conclusion

Egregious knavery is seldom practised, and would be rarer yet if the integrity of potential clients were always verified beforehand. Even when grim experiences become public knowledge, merchants who see themselves as endowed with superior cunning or luck will choose to disregard these warnings.

Flagrant misconduct is less worrisome to the trade, than controversies between people of goodwill. These arise when particular and standard contracts are silent on an important point, when a clause is incomplete or ambiguous or when a rule has become obsolete. The time wasted in fruitless conversations and telexes is worthy of a more profitable cause.

Knowledge of contracts and trade usage is indispensable to keeping out of trouble and to finding the correct answers. But a doctrinaire reliance on technicalities—however well-thought out—is self-defeating, where there is genuine doubt as to the construction of a term, and where both sides are in good faith. A forthcoming attitude toward like-minded trading partners, is desirable, from the practical and ethical standpoint. Agreements—and not just the small print—are a dead letter without the desire to keep one's word.

Bibliography

The only way to acquire expert knowledge in contracts, is to study them. The forms may be purchased from the associations issuing them:

The Grain and Feed Trade Association,
28 St. Mary Axe, London, EC3A 8EP, England.

F.O.S.F.A. International,
24 St. Mary Axe, London, EC3A 8ER, England.

North American Export Grain Association,
Suite 610 North, 1800 M Street N.W., Washington, D.C., 20036.

For the distinctions between delivery terms f.o.b., c. and f. and c.i.f. terms and their effect in English law, see David M. Sassoon, *C.I.F. and F.O.B. Contracts*, 2nd ed. *British Shipping Laws*, Vol. 5, (London: Stevens & Sons, 1975). See also *Guide to Incoterms* and *Incoterms International Rules for the Interpretation of Trade Terms*, publications with lively modernistic illustrations issued by the International Chamber of Commerce.

For the study of letters of credit, see *Uniform Customs and Practice for Documentary Credits*, also published by the International Chamber of Commerce. Copies of this publication may be obtained through the letter of credit departments of most large commercial banks, a number of which also issue their own booklets explaining commercial letters of credit. A revision of the *Customs* becomes effective in October 1984.

The serious student of contracts must follow legal developments in *Lloyd's Law Reports*, where a surprising number of cases involve commodity and maritime transactions.

The authoritative English text prior to the 1979 Arbitration Act, was *Russell on Arbitration*, 18th ed., rev. by Anthony Walton, Q.C. (London: Stevens & Sons Ltd., 1970). The current text is *The Law and Practice of Commercial Arbitration in England* by Sir Michael J. Mustill and Stewart C. Boyd, London, Butterworths 1982. The standard American work on arbitration is *Domke on Commercial Arbitration* (*The Law and Practice of Commercial Arbitration*). Revised edition by Gabriel M. Wilmer, Chicago, Callaghan and Co., 1984, published in loose-leaf form.

Unfortunately, commodity arbitration awards are not made accessible, unless they are cited when under review by courts of law. Maritime arbitrations held under the auspices of the New York Society of Maritime Arbitrators, however, are reported in full. These awards afford invaluable insights into the facts, the issues, the contentions of the parties, and the reasoning of the arbitrators. The service may be subscribed to with the Society which also prints a small journal, *The Arbitrator*, with thoughtful and up-to-date articles on maritime cases and arbitration in general.

An interesting compendium of articles on arbitral questions of current interest, is *The Art of Arbitration, Essays on International—Arbitration Liber Amicorum Pieter Sanders*, Eds., Jan C. Schultsz, Albert Jan van den Berg (Deventer, Netherlands: Kluwer Law and Taxation Publishers, 1982).

The definitive work on charterparty law is *Scrutton on Charterparties and Bills of Lading*, 18th ed., by Sir Alan Abraham Mocatta, Michael J. Mustill and Stewart C. Boyd, London, Sweet and Maxwell, 1974. The quality of English commercial jurisprudence may be gauged by the fact that Mr. Justice Mustill is co-author of the authoritative works on arbitration as well as on charterparties.

Index